HAMLYN All-colour ENCYCLOPEDIAS

Man's Wonderful World

Hamlyn

London · New York · Sydney · Toronto

Published 1978 by
The Hamlyn Publishing Group Limited
London · New York · Sydney · Toronto
Astronaut House, Feltham, Middlesex, England

ISBN 0 600 36327 9

Printed in Czechoslovakia

The material in this book appeared originally in *The Hamlyn
Junior Encyclopedia of Nature*, *The Hamlyn Junior Science
Encyclopedia* and *The Hamlyn Younger Children's Encyclopedia*.
51137

Contents

The history of man

Early man

It is only in the last few hundred years that man has come to realise how small he is in the vast expanse of the universe. Science has taught him that the earth he lives on is like a mere speck of dust in the air. And the span of man's life on earth is very short compared with the estimated age of the planet. The earth was formed about 5,000 million years ago but man has lived on it for only about 500,000 years. In other words, if the whole period of the earth's life was divided into 10,000 equal parts, man would have existed for only one of them.

The other fact about man which is now accepted by nearly everyone is that he is part of the great chain of life which began on earth thousands of millions of years ago. He has evolved, or developed, within the animal kingdom and is classified as a mammal. He belongs to the group called primates, which includes the apes and monkeys, to which he is related. Most biologists believe that man and the ape had a common ancestor.

The fossil remains of bones, skulls, tools and weapons buried in the earth and discovered by scientists have made it possible for many of the

Below Man is a meat-eating creature and he used to hunt for his food. In the early days of his existence, he had to use primitive weapons like clubs and lumps of rock.

clothing made from skins. Man's first permanent homes were caves, and it was about 10–12,000 years ago that the famous cave paintings of animals and people, discovered in France and Spain, were done.

The term Stone Age (usually divided into three periods, called Old, Middle and New) does not apply to a fixed period of time. When the early civilisations of the ancient world were very advanced and highly organised, people in Britain were still living in the Stone Age. In the same way, certain primitive people still live in Stone Age conditions today, and it is possible to see the way man behaved thousands of years ago by studying the everyday life of such people.

The Ice Ages were periods when large areas of the globe were covered with ice. They began about 1 million years ago. When the last of them was over, about 10,000 years ago, and the land became warmer again, man began to settle down and live by farming. The practice of agriculture formed the basis for society as we know it today, and it first began in the fertile valleys of Egypt and Mesopotamia.

various stages of man's development to be plotted. But there are still missing links and it is not easy to decide which animal was the first true man. Certainly, man is the most successful of all animals. He has a large and complex brain, can use tools, has the power of speech and the ability to reason. He has adapted himself to live in almost every natural condition found on earth, and in space itself.

The oldest man-like primates are called australopithecines, and they lived in southern Africa from 1–2 millions years ago. They were probably cave-dwellers and may have used simple tools. About 500,000 years ago more developed creatures such as Java Man and Peking Man existed. There is evidence that they used fire for heating and cooking. Neanderthal Man lived in parts of Europe about 100,000 years ago, and was skilled in the use of weapons and tools.

Man, as a tool-making animal, was given the name *Homo sapiens*, or 'Man, the wise one'. During the Old Stone Age, before the discovery of metal, he wandered about from place to place, living 'off the land', hunting animals, eating wild vegetation and learning to fish. These early men probably had rough shelters and some form of

River valley civilisations

History begins only with the records man was able to leave behind him. The earliest civilisations grew up around four great river valleys: the Tigris/Euphrates in Mesopotamia, the Nile in Egypt, the Yellow River in China and the Indus in India. In these places, so far as we know, men first created organised societies and, what is most important, made lasting records of what they did.

Above **The earliest Egyptian boats were made from bundles of papyrus reeds tied together.**

Key dates in world history
4000 BC Sumerians established on Plain of Shinar.
3500 BC Sumerian cities, Ur, Erech etc. established.
3400 BC Upper and Lower Egypt joined. 1st Dynasty.
2500/1500 BC Indus valley civilisation.
2500/1400 BC Minoan civilisation in Crete.
1760/1122 BC Shang Dynasty in China.
1750/550 BC Persian Empire.
1225 BC Israelites leave Egypt.
1100/612 BC Assyrian Empire.

Above **Wall paintings found at Knossos, capital of an ancient civilisation on the island of Crete, suggest that athletes performed a dangerous form of bull-baiting as a popular public entertainment.**

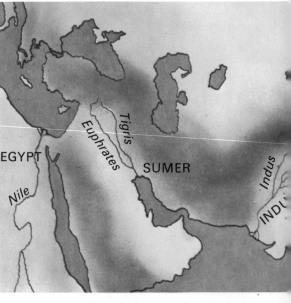

This hunting scene is based on a wall carving made in the 9th century BC from the palace of King Assurnasipal at Nimrud in ancient Assyria.

No one can give an exact date when these civilisations began. As with every stage of man's development, the formation of these civilisations took a long time; the gradual coming together of people into social groups on a large scale, however, is thought to have happened about 5000 BC. The Indus valley civilisations at Mohenjo-daro and Harappa in India are later, perhaps about 2500 BC; and there are no records before the beginning of the Shang dynasty, about 1750 BC, of Chinese civilisation, although it goes further back than this.

Mesopotamia, which means 'the land between two rivers', was known in ancient times as Sumer, and its people as Sumerians. It was an area of independent city-states, the most famous of which is Ur. The people who first settled there came from the flat, high country we now know as Iran, or Persia. They were already farmers and they began to cultivate isolated areas of fertile land where the earth was rich. As these communities grew, the city-states did not band together but lived in a state of constant war with each other.

The Sumerians were skilled metal workers, particularly in bronze, which is an alloy (mixture) of tin and copper: this is why the period is often called the Bronze Age. The Sumerians were also one of the first peoples to use writing. They invented a system called cuneiform, in which marks were made on soft clay with a stylus, because they needed to keep a record of their possessions and such things as taxes collected from the people.

The first true nation was Egypt. Here the conditions for early settlement were roughly the same as in Mesopotamia, and life was centred around a great river, the Nile. Each year, rain on the tall mountains of Ethiopia, through which the Nile passes, causes the river to flood. This leaves a top layer of rich, black mud on the land in which crops grow well.

Above **The headdress of a Sumerian queen discovered in the royal tomb at Ur.**

Above **The archers of King Darius are pictured on enamelled tiles on the palace at Susa (6th century BC).**

River Valley Civilisations

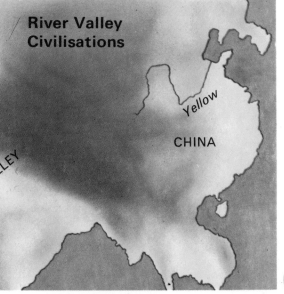

Yellow

CHINA

ALLEY

Right **A three-legged bronze cauldron dating from the Shang dynasty in China.**

Below **This bronze figure of a dancing girl was made by people of the Indus valley about 4,000 years ago.**

At first, the floods did not go down naturally and some way of distributing the water had to be found. This need for irrigation (a system for watering the land) made the people work together for the common good, and it was this fact, more than any other, which probably led to the first united nation of people.

Egypt was made up of two distinct areas. The oldest part, called Lower Egypt, was the rich delta land where the Nile branches out and flows into the Mediterranean. Upper Egypt ran from the delta along the narrow valleys which follow the course of the Nile, to Aswan in the south. The history of

Egypt really begins about 3400 BC when the two lands were united under one king, called the pharaoh. He ruled from Memphis and his symbol of power was the double crown, which combined the white crown of Upper Egypt with the red crown of Lower Egypt.

The early people of China and India also depended on the fertile land of river valleys. The Chinese discovered for themselves many of the things which had been 'invented' in Egypt and Mesopotamia. The most striking thing about the early cities of India is their carefully planned streets and buildings and their 'modern' drainage system.

Above **The ruins of Athena's temple – the Parthenon – on the Acropolis in Athens.**

490–480 BC Greeks defeat Persians
c. 450 BC Great age of Athenian leader, Pericles
431–404 BC Peloponnesian War
336–323 BC Alexander of Macedon extends Greek empire
146 BC Romans destroy Carthage
55–54 BC Caesar invades Britain
c. 4 BC Birth of Jesus Christ
AD 43 Roman conquest of Britain begins
117 Hadrian rules in Rome, Roman Empire at its greatest
330 Constantine founds Constantinople
455 Vandals sack Rome

Below **Rival city states of Athens and Sparta were constantly at war during the 5th century BC.**

Greeks and Romans

The first wandering tribes to settle in in the mountain peninsula of Greece came from the north about 2000 BC. They were an Indo-European people called the Achaeans. Before they came, highly developed civilisations existed in some of the islands in the Aegean Sea, on the coast of Asia Minor (where ancient Troy was situated) and, most important of all, on the island of Crete, where the Minoans already had links with the older civilisations of Egypt and Mesopotamia. Early Greece owes a great deal to the Minoans, who were mysteriously wiped out by a fire which swept the island about 1400 BC.

Because Greece has a chain of mountains running down its spine and its coastline is cut into a jagged

Below **This map shows how the Roman Empire expanded until, at the height of its power in AD 117, it included all the lands around the Mediterranean Sea.**

Above **Pericles, the most brilliant statesman of the Golden Age of Greece, had the temples on the Acropolis built.**

Below **A golden funeral mask found at Mycenae by the German archaeologist Heinrich Schliemann. He called it the 'Mask of Agamemnon'.**

Below **Here is an example of early Greek jewellery. It is part of a gold belt from Thessaly and is dated about the 3rd century BC.**

R. Rhine
R. Danube
Rome
Troy
Athens
Sparta
Syracuse
R. Nile

Roman Empire about AD117

pattern of inlets by the sea, it was often difficult for people in one place to communicate with those in another. This is one of the reasons why Greece became a country of city-states, such as Athens, Thebes and Sparta.

Although Greece was split into self-governing city-states, the people were bound together by many beliefs and traditions which they had in common. This was the origin of the Greek spirit, which was based on a fierce feeling for personal independence. At first, the city-states were ruled by kings but gradually a system grew up called democracy (a word which comes from the Greek for 'people', *demos*). Unlike 'democracies' in the modern world the Greek city-state was a small unit. Athens,

Above **This is the ruin of the Colosseum which was a Roman amphitheatre built in AD 72–80. It was in the Colosseum that the gladiators would fight wild animals. The first games held there lasted a hundred days and thousands of men and beasts were killed.**

Below **A Roman aqueduct at Segovia in Spain.**

for example, had only about 40,000 citizens and of these every freeman was entitled to speak and vote at meetings of the Assembly, or parliament. So the Greeks did not elect other people to represent them, but each freeman took a personal part in government.

During the greatest period of Greek history, in the 5th century BC, called the 'classical' period, Athens was the centre of the world. It was at this time that the temples of the Acropolis, which exist today as noble ruins, were built under the direction of the great leader, Pericles. The art, literature, science and philosophy of the 'classical' Greek period have had more influence on western civilisation than that of any other period in the history of man.

The Peloponnesian War (431–404 BC) between Athens and her fellow city-state, Sparta, sapped their strength and allowed Philip of Macedon to take over the leadership of all Greece. His son Alexander succeeded him and in a series of brilliant campaigns extended the Macedonian empire and spread Greek civilisation to the frontiers of the then-known world.

The power of Greece passed eventually to Rome. At the time of Alexander the Great, this Italian city already controlled the whole of Italy. She was then to engage in a bitter struggle with Carthage in the Punic Wars which lasted, on and off, for over 100 years. Rome emerged the victor and spread her entire empire along the shores of north Africa and to the coasts of Britain.

The Greeks had given the world great art and thinking; the Romans, who were practical men, gave it good government and good laws. Wherever the Romans went on their conquests they tried to allow the people as much freedom as possible, while encouraging them to live in the Roman way. The Romans were also great engineers and evidence of the long-lasting strength of their buildings can still be seen all over Europe. Roman rule lasted for about 500 years and it brought many benefits to people within the Empire. There was a time in the 1st and 2nd centuries AD when for nearly 100 years there was no war and the whole world was at peace.

The Dark Ages

Below **Early books were hand written by monks. They were beautifully decorated with bright colours and gold leaf.**

The Dark Ages is the name given to a period of history following the collapse of the Roman Empire, when western civilisation was overrun and Christian ideas were challenged by the barbarians. Who were these barbarians and where did they come from? The word 'barbarian' is Greek and means 'foreign', and the Romans applied it to anyone who did not share their way of life. The barbarian hordes were made up of a number of different races from the north and east of Europe and Asia. They included the Goths, Vandals, Franks, Saxons and, fiercest of them all, the Huns, who came from central Asia. They overran the western part of the old Roman Empire and brought a period of darkness to Europe.

476 Fall of Roman Empire in the West
563 St. Columba lands on Iona
570 Birth of Mohammed
597 St. Augustine's Christian mission to England
619 T'ang dynasty in China
622 Moslem religion founded
664 Synod of Whitby
711 Moslems invade Spain
800 Charlemagne crowned as Holy Roman Emperor
871 Alfred the Great, king of Wessex
c. 1000 Vikings discover Nova Scotia
1066 Battle of Hastings. William of Normandy becomes king of England

Left **These gilt bronze horses which now stand before St. Mark's Cathedral in Venice are part of Crusading history. They once stood on Trajan's Imperial Arch in Rome. Constantine took them to Constantinople, but when the city was attacked by Christian crusaders in 1204 the horses were moved to Venice.**

Below **This is a Viking longship built about the 10th century. It was in warships like this that the Vikings invaded Britain and western Europe between the 8th and 10th centuries.**

One of the most important dates in the history of the breakdown of Roman power is AD 364, when the Empire was split into two parts. In AD 330 the emperor Constantine had already moved the capital to Byzantium in Asia Minor and renamed it Constantinople. Then it was decided that the Empire was too big to govern from one place and two capitals, one in the east and one in the west, were set up. This and other signs of weakness were seized upon by the barbarian tribes in the north who were eager to attack Rome.

Only in the monasteries were the traditions of learning guarded. In AD 380 the emperor Theodosius I had decreed that Christianity should be the official religion of the Roman state. Even before this the Christian faith had spread to the outermost limits of the Roman Empire, where it had developed and flourished in spite of the confusion of the Dark Ages.

Despite the invasions, during the next two centuries the power of Christianity grew and the Bishop of Rome, whom Christians believed had inherited the mantle of St. Peter himself, became known as pope, or father, of the Catholic Church. Pope Gregory sent St. Augustine to England in AD 597 to bring the pagan Saxons back to the Christianity which the British had known in Roman times. On the continent of Europe the warrior-king Charlemagne came to the throne and in AD 800 founded the Holy Roman Empire, which united large areas of central Europe and lasted for 1,000 years.

The pagan people of north Germany made a final bid to challenge the Christian world of the west when the Vikings, or Danes, attacked Europe's coasts and rivers from the sea. This 'Viking Age' lasted from the 8th to the 10th centuries, and after many fierce battles the Vikings settled in the lands they had come to conquer and became a part of them. In England, the Danish invaders mixed easily with the Saxons who had taken over the country after the fall of the Roman Empire, for they had many of the same customs. The final settlement of the Vikings came when Canute became

Below (1) Saracens fighting Christians in the Crusades. (2) shows a Saracen sword which could be opened up like scissors. Armour once had jewels on it like this Celtic shield (3). King Alfred's jewel is seen in (4).

Above Here is a typical Viking warrior of the 10th century. The Vikings were clever seafarers and brave soldiers who served as a volunteer army under leaders of great ability. They were very well disciplined but brutal and were allowed to keep what they had looted from those they had captured or killed.

king of England in 1017 and for a time ruled over England, Denmark and Norway.

Another great event of the Dark Ages was the coming of the Arab peoples upon the scene of world history. In the 7th century Mohammed became the prophet of God and united the Arab people in one faith. Their conquests, which were spurred on by a burning desire to convert the whole world, extended over the Middle East, along the coast of north Africa and into Spain.

15

Above **The jousting tournaments of medieval knights provided a very entertaining sport. Sometimes, however, they were fought in earnest and the lance became a lethal weapon.**

The medieval world

During their campaigns in the Middle East the Arabs captured Jerusalem, the Holy City of Christianity. At a Council in 1095, Pope Urban II called upon the Christian knights of Europe to band together in a great fighting Crusade to recapture the city. This led to a series of Crusades in which there were many brutal battles but few positive results. Jerusalem was taken by the Christian armies in the first Crusade, only to be re-taken by the Arab sultan, Saladin, after which it remained an Islamic city until the Allied armies captured it during the First World War in 1917.

After the barbarian invasions had died away and the northern peoples had found a place in western society, life in Europe was based on a way of government called the feudal system. The word 'feudal' comes from the Latin, meaning 'a fief', which is an area of land held by someone in return for service, either in the fields or as a soldier in time of war.

The most important thing to everyone was the land, and farming occupied the mass of the people. The peasants were poor and their lives and property belonged to a local lord. They tilled the land and produced food for themselves and for their master, in return for his protection. Each district, or manor, had its village, church, manor house and mill, set amid woods and pastureland.

The lord of the manor was usually a knight, and he in turn was a tenant or vassal of one of the powerful

Above **Salisbury Cathedral is built in the Gothic style.**

Below right **Medieval towns had cobbled streets and overhanging wooden houses like this.**

Right **Here is Edward, the Black Prince, son of Edward III.**

Far left **These are Lombards who were bankers from Italy.**

Below **A map showing the Third Crusade of 1189. Its aim was to defeat Saladin and win back Jerusalem from the Moslems. Three important European rulers took part— Richard I (the Lion-heart) of England; Philip II of France and Frederick Barbarossa of Germany. Frederick was drowned on his way to the Holy Land.**

1095 First Crusade
1099 Capture of Jerusalem by Christian armies
1170 Murder of Becket
1187 Saladin captures Jerusalem
1215 Magna Carta signed
1260 Kublai Khan conquers China
1290 Jews expelled from England
1338 Beginning of 100 Years War
1349 Black Death
1415 Battle of Agincourt
c. 1200–1400 Hanseatic League of German cities
1431 Execution of Joan of Arc
1206 Genghis Khan founds Mongol Empire

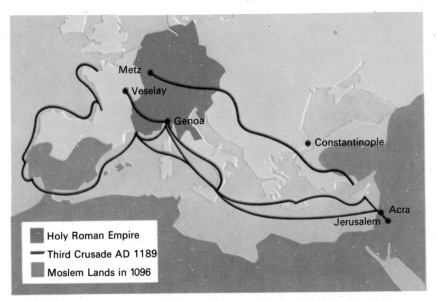

Metz
Veselay
Genoa
Constantinople
Acra
Jerusalem

Holy Roman Empire
Third Crusade AD 1189
Moslem Lands in 1096

barons who controlled the country on behalf of the king. Even so, the peasants, or serfs, were not allowed to leave the district or even get married, without the lord's permission. This meant that conditions for the peasant in the Middle Ages depended upon what kind of master he had. If the lord was just, things were bearable, but if he was not then life was hard and miserable.

The peasants' lot began to improve when it became the custom to allow them to pay their lords money instead of working for them. The most dramatic event in the Middle Ages, which affected the peasants' lives more than anything else, was the Black Death which swept across Europe in 1347–50, killing a third of the population. This meant that there were many more jobs available than men to fill them. Wages rose and so did the peasants' standard of living.

The Crusades lasted for about 200 years. This encouraged the profession of knighthood, and when the knights were not fighting the infidel abroad, they fought among themselves, either in serious battles or in mock tournaments. The sons of noblemen were trained not only to fight with lance and sword, but to be chivalrous and well-spoken and to behave in a

Above **A peasant scene by the Flemish artist, Peter Bruegel.**

Below **Many noblemen retained minstrels to entertain them.**

Bottom **Medieval lovers swore undying faith to their ladies.**

'knightly' fashion. When they had grown up to be proper knights they took serious vows to serve God and be true and valiant.

Everyday life in the Middle Ages was ruled not only by the knights and barons but by the Church. Each village had its place of worship and its priest, and the religious festivals were the only holidays the peasants had. As well as the parish churches there were the many large monasteries which grew up at this time. Into them the monks withdrew to lead a self-contained life of worship away from the world. But many of these same monks also looked after people by teaching them and caring for the sick. They also kept alive the tradition of art and learning as it was practised in the classical world, until it flowered again in the Renaissance.

Renaissance and Reformation

Towards the end of the Middle Ages, merchants began to take the place of knights, and commerce became more important than wars of honour and glory. As men moved about more from place to place, the traders of Europe became a powerful new class. Cities grew in strength and importance upon the basis of trade, and the fortunes of the principal Italian city-states – Venice, Florence, Rome, Milan – all at the very heart of the movement known as the Renaissance, were gathered from trade.

The Renaissance has been called the greatest period in the history of art and man. The word Renaissance means rebirth, and it is used principally to apply to the new surge of interest in the arts and in the importance of man as an individual. It was an age which looked back to the classical era of Greece and Rome for its inspiration. It developed in Italy in the 15th century and during the 16th spread to the rest of Europe.

One astonishing thing about works of art in the Renaissance is their universal appeal. Every age and every culture recognises the genius of Michelangelo and Leonardo da Vinci. Much of their work and that of other great artists of the period was done against a background of conflict, cruelty and great social change. It could not have existed without the rich patronage of the popes and monarchs of that extravagant age.

Above **Henry VIII met Francis I of France in 1520 on the Field of the Cloth of Gold to settle disputes between them.**

Below **These pictures show (1) Charles V the Holy Roman Emperor; (2) Frederick the Wise and (3) Pope Paul III.**

Yet these artists speak directly from the heart to all men in every place and at any time.

Gutenberg's mid-15th-century invention of movable type and the growth of printing meant that knowledge, in the shape of printed books, was available to more people. Libraries were set up and households began to be able to afford a row of books on their shelves. Education spread and with it, curiosity. As well as being a period of rebirth in the arts and learning, the Renaissance produced men who were prepared to challenge the narrow traditional views of mankind and the universe. They were the scientists and explorers who trod new ground, either in the minds of men or on the shores of undiscovered lands.

Alongside the Renaissance there grew up a great challenge to the single authority of the Catholic Church in Rome. In medieval times Christianity had succeeded not only in spreading its message throughout the civilised world but in remaining united. Now a movement which came to be known as the Reformation caused many churchmen to break with Rome. One reason for this was that the Church had become rich, imposing taxes on poor people, and also the fact that several of the bishops, who in turn filled the office of pope, had become too involved with matters of state and were not good men.

The chief voice raised against the authority of the Church was that of

Right **Sir Thomas More, Lord Chancellor of England, who would not recognise Henry VIII as head of the English Church. He was arrested on a charge of treason and beheaded in 1535.**

Martin Luther, a German monk, who openly challenged Rome in a practical way by pinning up on the door of a church in Wittenburg a paper which listed 95 points on which he claimed the Church was wrong. He and his followers set up a rival 'reformed' church and because the chief reason for doing this was one of protest, the upholders of the new faith became known as Protestants.

Another strong feeling that grew up around the time of the Renaissance was the feeling for nationhood. Out of the confused state of Europe in the Middle Ages separate nations emerged, the first and most important being England, France and Spain.

Below **Martin Luther a German religious reformer of the 16th century.**

Below left **A page from Gutenberg's 42-line Bible.**

Above **Johann Gutenberg was the first man to use moveable type in Europe. Here he is printing his Bible.**

Exploration and discovery

The age of expansion, when the frontiers of the world were extended beyond Europe and the Mediterranean lands, began at the end of the 15th century. This reaching out across unknown seas was led by Portugal. In 1418 the wealthy nobleman, Prince Henry of Portugal, began his life-long interest in exploration and discovery, which gave his country the finest ships and seamen in the world. He spent money freely in paying for expeditions and improving methods of shipbuilding and systems of navigation. The first quest was for a sea route to the East, and for years his tiny ships

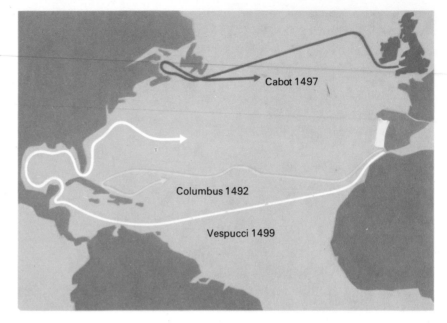

1468	Renaissance of art at its height in Italy
1478	Inquisition begins in Spain
1486	Diaz rounds Cape of Good Hope
1492	Columbus lands in West Indies
1493	Moors defeated at Granada in Spain
1509	Accession of Henry VIII of England
1519	First circumnavigation of the world
1535	First English printed Bible
1558	Accession of Elizabeth I as queen of England
1571	Battle of Lepanto
1572	Massacre of Hugenots on St. Bartholomew's Day
1588	Spanish Armada defeated
1603	Union of the crown of England and Scotland
1620	*Mayflower* sails to America
1643	Louis XIV, king of France
1694	Bank of England founded
1696	Peter the Great, czar of Russia
1704	Battle of Blenheim
1759	Wolfe takes Quebec

Above **This map shows the voyages of Cabot from England to Nova Scotia, 1497; of Vespucci to America, 1499 and of Columbus to the West Indies, 1492.**

Below **The Puritans were English Protestants who did not think the Reformation had gone far enough in doing away with rituals of the Catholic Church. A group of them joined the Pilgrim Fathers and sailed in 1620 to America so that they could practise their religion in peace. Here they are seen disembarking from their ship, the 'Mayflower', on to the shores of New England.**

tried again and again to sail their way along the west coast of Africa.

It was after Prince Henry's death that Bartholomew Diaz finally found a way round the Cape of Good Hope, at the southern tip of Africa. This was in 1488, and before the end of the century Columbus (in 1492) had made his landfall in the West Indies, Cabot had reached Newfoundland (1497) and Vespucci had explored the northern coast of South America (1499).

This series of landings in the Americas brought Europe into contact with the New World. At the beginning of the 16th century voyages were undertaken in greater number with the object of securing new territories. The Spanish soldiers, Cortes and Pizarro, uncovered the unknown civilizations of the Aztecs in Mexico and the Incas in Peru. The first successful journey right round the world was made in 1519–22 by Magellan's expedition, although he himself was killed during the voyage. Merchant adventurers scoured the seas for new areas of trade and profit.

In the period between the end of the 15th century and the middle of the 17th, not only were new areas of the world opened up, but individual nations grew stronger and fought with each other over the new lands. Command of the seas meant home shores were safe from invasion. This was to be shown dramatically in the defeat of the Spanish Armada by the English fleet whose captains' superior seamanship won the day.

In England, particularly, the Elizabethan age saw a glittering procession of great statesmen, sailors and poets who brought fame and fortune to their country. Sir Humphrey Gilbert and Sir Walter Raleigh attempted to found colonies on the East coast of North America and so built the foundations of Britain's empire.

After the conquest of Central and South America by Spain and Portugal, the continent of North America was colonised by several European powers, chiefly Britain and France. The coastal areas, rivers and lakes were explored by the French, and in

Below **Here Hernando Cortes is seen in Mexico with some Aztec Indians whom he massacred brutally.**

1608 Champlain founded Quebec. The Pilgrim Fathers settled in New England in 1620. They were a company of Puritan exiles who sailed from Plymouth in England in the *Mayflower* to find a new home where they were free to practise their religion.

The British extended their rule in India through the East India Company, which was founded in 1600 to exploit the country's resources. In Australia, colonisation began in 1788 when the first batch of convicts sentenced to transportation were landed in New South Wales. The Dutch built up an empire based on trade in the East Indies during the 17th century, and the French settled in south-east Asia.

The 17th century has been called the 'golden age of France'. She was prosperous and powerful under the rule of an absolute monarch, Louis XIV. This concentration of power in the king led directly to the French Revolution in 1789.

Above **Christopher Columbus** who sailed in 1492 to find a western route to India but found the West Indies instead.

Below **The search for gold was one reason why so many voyages of discovery were made. This picture shows Spanish soldiers fighting pirates who were constantly plundering ships carrying gold and other valuable treasures.**

Left **Sir Francis Drake (1540?–96) was the first Englishman to sail round the world.**

Far left **This is a medal commemorating Drake's voyage.**

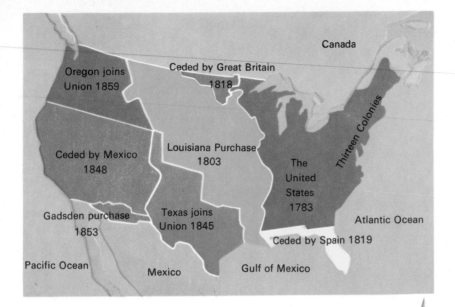

Above **Map showing how Americans gained control of their continent from the thirteen colonies along the Atlantic coast to the Pacific ocean.**

1764 Beginnings of Industrial Revolution
1776 American Declaration of Independence
1783 Treaty of Versailles
1789 French Revolution
1801 Union of Great Britain and N. Ireland
1804 Napoleon emperor of France
1805 Battle of Trafalgar Death of Nelson
1808 Peninsular War
1812 Napoleon's armies retreat from Moscow
1854/6 Crimean War
1857 Indian Mutiny
1861/5 American Civil War
1889/1902 South African War
1901 Death of Queen Victoria

Revolution and new ideas

At the time of the Revolution in France, the country was ruled by an all-powerful king and even the nobles had little part in the government of the country. They led an extravagant life at the royal court, paid no taxes, and had nothing to do with the common people. The prosperous merchants and bankers and, of course, the peasants, paid the taxes which allowed the king and his aristocratic court to lead their life of luxury. In 1789, Louis XVI decided to summon the States General, France's parliament, which had not met for 175 years. He was short of money and needed them to agree to new taxes. But the harvests had been bad for several years and the streets of Paris were full of people demanding food.

The king's last minute attempts to try and settle the unrest in his country

Below **Napoleon, emperor of France and, for a time, master of Europe.**

failed. It was too late to hold back the tide of feeling which was to sweep the king from his throne. On 14th July, 1789 a mob stormed the Bastille, the royal prison in Paris. This was the beginning of a wave of violence which spread over the whole country. In 1792 the common people had won and France became a republic. There followed a 'reign of terror' when the revolutionaries sent thousands of aristocrats, including the king and his queen, Marie Antoinette, to be beheaded by the newly-invented guillotine.

The Revolution ended the monarchy in France but out of the chaos which followed it created a new emperor – Napoleon. Between 1799 and 1815, when his armies were finally crushed at the Battle of Waterloo by the

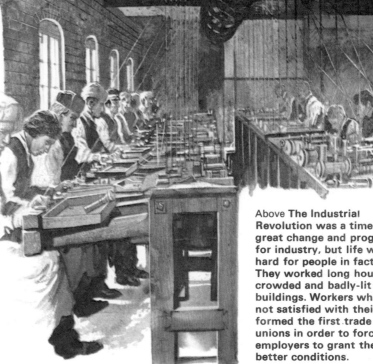

Above **The Industrial Revolution was a time of great change and progress for industry, but life was hard for people in factories. They worked long hours in crowded and badly-lit buildings. Workers who were not satisfied with their lot formed the first trade unions in order to force employers to grant them better conditions.**

Far left **The soldier in the foreground is wearing the uniform of the Union Army at the time of the Civil War in the United States, while the two men in the background show the more casual dress of the southern Confederacy. Alongside is a portrait of Abraham Lincoln.** Below left **are two scenes from the French Revolution: the storming of the Bastille, the royal prison in Paris; and an execution performed by the dreaded guillotine.**

Below **The picture shows Nelson at the Battle of Trafalgar. The sailor is hoisting Nelson's famous message to his men: England expects that every man will do his duty.**

British and the Prussians, Napoleon dominated Europe.

Britain was at war with France for most of the 18th century and in Canada there was a constant struggle between the two countries. In 1759 General Wolfe and the British forces won Quebec in a surprise attack and went on to capture Montreal. Canada submitted to British rule but the thirteen colonies in North America, which were to become the original United States, rebelled against long-distance government from Britain.

The War of Independence between Britain and the colonists had been in progress for a year when the Declaration of Independence, which has remained the charter of American liberties ever since, was drawn up in 1776 by Jefferson, Franklin and other American statesmen. George Washington led the revolt and with the help of the French triumphed over the British forces. Britain recognised the United States of America as an independent country in 1783 and Washington became its first president.

During the next 70 years the American pioneers pushed westwards across their vast continent to the Pacific Ocean and established their northern boundary with Canada. Because some of the states believed in slave labour and others did not, a Civil War resulted between south and north. It lasted for four years (1861–5)

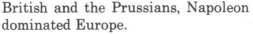

Above **In the early days of Communism, Lenin was a leading member of the Bolshevik party. After the Russian Revolution in 1917 and the overthrow of the provisional government which had been set up, Lenin was elected president of the first Soviet government.**

and ended with victory for Lincoln and the northern armies.

The Industrial Revolution, a period of great technical advance, began in Britain in the 18th century. It revolutionised industry by the introduction of new methods and machines. Britain was changed from an agricultural community to an industrial one, and similar developments took place later all over Europe and in the United States. In the 19th century Britain's industrial strength coincided with her greatest period of political power.

Two world wars

Man has made war against man probably since the beginning of his time on earth. But only in the 20th century have the weapons of mass destruction been so efficient and so terrible. In a curious and hopeful way the very power of modern weapons has made their use less likely – for no nation could hope to escape the consequences of an all-out attack.

The First World War (1914–18) happened because the nations of Europe were envious and frightened of one another. Ever since 1900 they had spent large sums of money arming themselves and making treaties so that different powers became grouped together as allies. The single event which sparked off the fighting seemed

Above **Three military leaders of the 1939–45 war – (1) Field Marshal Montgomery; (2) Field Marshal Rommel and (3) General Eisenhower.**

1914	Outbreak of First World War
1915	Gallipoli campaign
1916	Battle of Jutland
1916	Battle of the Somme
1917	Revolution in Russia
1918	Armistice signed
1922	Irish Free State founded
1924	First Labour government in Britain
1933	Hitler comes to power in Germany
1936	Civil War in Spain
1939	Outbreak of Second World War
1940	Evacuation of British army from Dunkirk
1941	Japanese attack on Pearl Harbour
1944	Allied armies land in France
1945	Germany and Japan surrender

Below **Tanks are an essential feature of modern warfare. At the beginning of the First World War, armoured cars had been used but their wheels could not cross the trenches. After the invention of caterpillar tracks, the tank was evolved. Britain's secret weapon first appeared in 1916 in Flanders. The picture shows the British Mark I tank.**

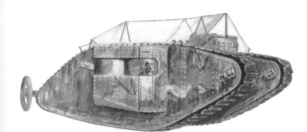

unimportant at the time but it set in motion a chain of events which no one seemed able to halt.

Archduke Ferdinand, heir to the Austrian throne, was murdered in Serbia in June, 1914. Austria declared war on Serbia, and Russia came in on the side of Serbia. Germany declared war on Russia and invaded Belgium and France and because of Britain's previous promises to aid those countries, she joined Belgium and France. America entered the war on the side of the Allies in 1917.

At first, everyone went to war with enthusiasm and said 'it will be over by Christmas'. In fact, the 'Great War' dragged on for four weary years, millions of men were killed and, in the light of what followed in Europe, solved very little.

Despite the determination of the Allied powers that there should never again be another war, the Second World War (1939–45) followed the

Above **A French 75 mm gun of the 1914–18 war.**

Below **The atom bomb, the first nuclear bomb ever to be used. When in 1945 one was dropped first on Hiroshima and then on Nagasaki, Japan immediately asked for an armistice.**

Left **A German tri-plane of the First World War, Richthofen's Fokker Dr.I.**

Above **War tactics were very different in the First World War from those used in the Second. In 1914–18 the troops dug themselves into trenches in the ground, firing at the enemy over the top. In the second war, there was much more movement of armies with a greater use of armoured vehicles.**

First, after a short and troubled period of only 20 years. Many will say that the peace terms imposed on Germany after the First World War made it certain that such a man as Adolf Hitler would appear, demanding to make his country strong again. This time, Germany, Italy and Japan lined up against Britain, France, the United States and Russia.

Unlike the First World War, in which troops spent years fighting over the same ground in France, there was very little trench warfare in the Second. It was a war of movement, of ships, aeroplanes and armoured vehicles, during which for a long period it seemed certain that Germany would win. It was also a war in which civilians were as exposed as the fighting men to danger and death. Massive air-raids took place on both sides, and it was from an aeroplane that the fearsome atomic bomb was unleashed by the Americans upon cities in Japan.

While the war was still in progress, Churchill and Roosevelt planned an Atlantic Charter of human rights and laid the foundations of the United Nations Organisation.

Below **Two fighter planes of the Second World War. The Vickers Supermarine Spitfire (in foreground) and the German Messerschmitt Me109.**

Below **A German 8·8 cm gun.**

Right **Field Marshal von Hindenburg who became Supreme Commander of the German Armies of the Eastern Front during the First World War.**

The modern world

All over the world there is social and scientific change, and everywhere patterns of conduct are being altered and old traditions discarded. A vast network of communications allows people of different cultures to come together, and the speed of modern transport is breaking down barriers that once existed. In this sense the world has become smaller, with many

nations uniting for the common good.

It has always been the aim of man to strive for a united world. As the ancient Greeks spread their influence through many lands, they tried to unite peoples by commissioning ambassadors to settle the questions of war and peace. Believing in a common culture they standardised such things as money, weights and measures. The Roman system was quite different, for they believed that people in the countries they had conquered should have their own individual cultures, although they all abided by a common law. This system worked successfully for about 500 years and there has since

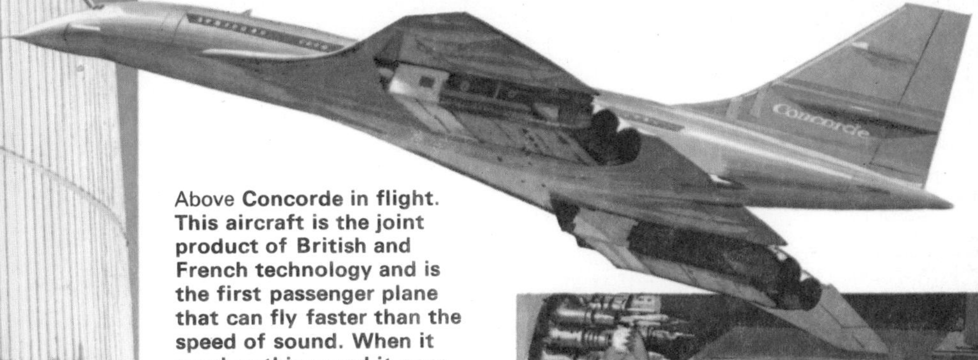

Above **Concorde** in flight. This aircraft is the joint product of British and French technology and is the first passenger plane that can fly faster than the speed of sound. When it reaches this speed it goes 'through the sound barrier' and makes a supersonic boom which can be heard on the ground.

Right **Computers**, which do much of the 'thinking' for man, are being used extensively in industry. This picture shows a large factory computer used for mass production.

4

5

Above **Two examples of the modern world – (4) the City Hall in Toronto, Canada, and (5) electronic machines which are now being used to teach children in day schools.**

Above **Although man is very clever, he has not yet learnt how to feed all the hungry people of the world. That is why hundreds of children like these are undernourished.**

been no world government to equal that of Rome.

Part of the world is a land of plenty, but there are still areas where people go hungry or have not kept pace with 20th-century developments. The fact that people unite to build dams, or to preserve animal life, or to study art and science, is a hopeful sign. Although the nations of the world draw closer together, they still exist under the fear of a third world war – this time with nuclear weapons.

After the Second World War, Germany was split into two halves by the victorious Allies. The East, which became known as the German Democratic Republic, came under the influence of the Soviet Union, while the West, known as the Federal Republic of Germany, was controlled by the Western Powers, mainly Britain and the United States. Berlin, which now lies in East Germany, was itself partitioned into East and West. The Soviet Union emerged as one of the two great world powers, the other being the United States. China too, another Communist power, has become of increasing international importance.

The United Nations Organisation was formed in 1945, so that the various nations of the world could put forward their points of view and argue out their differences of opinion. The powers of the Soviet Union and the United States are carefully balanced by military force and the possession of nuclear weapons and peace has been maintained. Both countries are trying now to bridge the gap between them. There is, for example, great co-operation in the field of space exploration. These are pointers to the world unity which must exist if mankind is to continue to survive.

Food from the land and sea

Grain crops are the most important sources of food from plants. They can be used directly as cereals and they also help feed the farm stock which provides man with meat and dairy produce.

With one or two exceptions, all the grain crops belong to the grass family. In temperate climates wheats are the chief cereals, the most important being the variety used for making bread, cakes, biscuits and pastry. Durum wheat is used for making pasta, and there are other varieties now used mainly as food for livestock, although they were once very important to man as food.

Rye, oats and barley are other cereals used extensively for human consumption. Corn is the only crop which is American in origin. Since it was brought to Europe by Columbus it has been dispersed to many other parts of the world. Corn, which is also

Right **The invention of the wheel made ploughing easier. This type of plough, although primitive, is still in use in some parts of the world today.**

Above **Modern farmers use combine harvesters which reap, thresh, winnow and bundle the straw in one operation.**

Left **A screw device for drawing water for irrigation. Compare the modern irrigation system in the picture below.**

called maize, is a good source of starch, but it has a lower protein value than the other grain crops.

Rice is one of the world's two most important food crops, the other being wheat. In countries where it is grown, rice provides a large proportion of the total amount of food eaten, so its value as a food is very high. Rice has been grown in China for nearly 5,000 years and it still dominates Chinese and other Asian agriculture. Rice growing in other continents is expanding steadily and it is now cultivated in Africa, South America, the United States and Australia on a commercial scale. Millets are grown in the tropics, for they can tolerate poor soil and drought. At the same time they have a high mineral content compared with other cereals.

Although all plants manufacture sugar, the sugar used by man comes mainly from sugar cane and sugar beet. Sugar is very important for it is an energy-producing food. Sugar gives its best yields in the tropics but it is also grown in the northern parts of the United States and in southern Spain.

Above **Fresh fruit is essential to us as it is a valuable source of vitamins. Oranges, which are one of the citrus fruits, grow in sunny climes. Other citrus fruits are limes, lemons and grapefruit.**

Above **These are some of our better-known cereals. They are important to us because they are made into flour and other items of food and provide us with starch and vitamins.**

Below **A modern dairy farming unit.**

Sugar beet is grown in the cooler temperate climates and although the plant was known in pre-Christian days, its use as a main sugar supply is a fairly modern development.

Coffee, chicory and tea are grown for use as beverages. Coffee is consumed by one-third of the world's population and tea by almost one-half. Although not of any special food value, these three beverages are important economically. Cocoa is another beverage which has a high food value.

Protein is essential to man's health and this comes mainly from beef, lamb and pork, which all come from animals bred by man to be eaten. Protein is also found in large quantities in fish. By far the greater part of the fish eaten as food is obtained from fish living in natural surroundings and caught with nets and lines. Fishing industries exist in every part of the world. Milk and cheese are other important sources of protein, so it is vital that the animals from which we obtain protein are, in turn, supplied with the right grain crops.

No plant can survive without water and as there is a shortage of food in the world, man is now taking pains to see that crops are grown even in areas where there is little water. To do this he uses various methods of irrigation to supply water to crops.

Below **Just as people in the West obtain starch from bread and potatoes, so in the East rice (left) is cultivated for the same purpose. It is grown in wet 'paddy' fields like the ones in the picture.**

Below **Three methods of obtaining food from the sea – (A) spear fishing; (B) dredge fishing and (C) trawler fishing.**

A

B

C

Cooking our food

Above **Early man roasting a fish in front of a fire.**

Before fire had been discovered, man ate his food raw. He hunted what he could and many people must have died through lack of the essential vitamins. It is believed that the burning of livestock in forest fires first gave man the idea of making fires to cook his food. When he was able to make use of fire, man probably just tossed a carcass into the middle of a fire and hauled it out when it was partly cooked. It is likely that many years passed before some prehistoric cook thought of skewering the meat and holding it over the flames.

In many primitive parts of the world ancient practices in cookery are still carried on. Although some civilisations had discovered how to preserve meat by drying and salting, it was the people of the eastern Mediterranean countries who studied food preparation as an art. The Greeks and Romans in particular were elaborate cooks.

Centuries passed and man ate a larger variety of foods, still cooked on open fires. People on the continent of Europe were eating cooked vegetables in the Middle Ages, while in Britain the pleasures of the table consisted of meat, pastry and sweetmeats. Medieval kitchens were very large and at banqueting time many cooks were employed. Cookshops were also in use at this time. They sold hot dishes or cooked customers' own food. Not until the 16th century did anyone seriously begin to plan kitchen aids.

The existence of vitamins in food was not established until 1912. This discovery was made by Sir Frederick Gowland Hopkins who demonstrated the presence of vitamins in milk. After this, studies of food and its value to man continued and we are now aware of the amounts of each type of food

Above **Dinner in an Elizabethan manor house. Only the rich could dine like this. Note the minstrel with his lute.**

Right **Some common herbs and flavourings. They are (1) mint; (2) garlic; (3) rosemary; (4) oregano; (5) bay; (6) parsley; (7) thyme; (8) mustard; (9) black pepper; (10) salt; (11) brown and white sugar; (12) root ginger.**

Far right **The Chinese do not use knives and forks but chopsticks instead. These are often made of bone, and are just as efficient as knives and forks.**

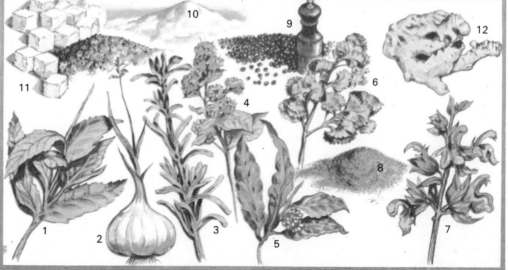

Above **A quick way to cook is with a frying pan.**

Above right **Grilling is better than frying as it preserves more of the food's flavour.**

Right **Poultry and joints of meat are roasted in ovens.**

Far right **Some foods have to be boiled in a saucepan.**

Below **How a side of beef is cut to make joints (1). The pieces of meat in the picture are (2) brisket of beef; (3) rolled sirloin of beef and (4) a piece of rump steak.**

needed to keep the body healthy. In the western world today it is rare for people to fall sick through lack of an essential food. Nevertheless, there is a world shortage of food and in less fortunate countries the people are grossly underfed.

Although most people do eat better food and are able to cook it on modern cookers, styles of cooking vary enormously. Food can be cooked by boiling, frying, grilling and roasting.

The British are fond of boiled meats and traditional steak and kidney pies and puddings, and stews. The Americans are renowned for their enormous steaks which are either fried or grilled, and in both countries roast joints of meat are popular. The French are also great beef-eaters. They cook it very lightly by frying or grilling, and garnish it with the most delicious sauces. They also use a great deal of butter in cooking. The Italians

love pasta and eat it in all shapes and forms, while the Spanish like to eat *paella* (a mixture of shellfish, chicken and rice), and cook their food in oil.

In Europe today there is a great interchange of recipes and it is not unusual for the people in one country to cook, as a matter of course, a traditional meal of another.

In eastern countries, rice, which is either boiled or fried, is the basic dish. The Chinese accompany their rice with pork, chicken or fish, and they have their own distinctive culinary vegetables which are always very finely sliced. They are masters at blending flavours together and Chinese food is enjoyed everywhere. In India rice is served with curried dishes containing spiced meats and vegetables.

Building through the ages

When man first lived in caves he wore no clothes and spoke no language. His life was concerned with finding food. But the climate of the world was changing and man was developing in intelligence and culture. In time, he began to set about making homes to shelter himself. Man became a builder, using wood and other natural materials. He made homes of grass and leaves, skins and logs. Even today, the Bantu tribes of Africa have houses which are very cleverly made of gras , reeds and branches.

The Bedouin, a people from the desert regions of Africa, live in tents made from cloth and animal hair. These homes are portable and are carried by the Bedouin to wherever they can find water. Other tent dwellers were the Red Indians of North America who lived in tents called tepees made of buffalo skins. Similar to the tepees of the Red Indians are the tents of the people called Samoyeds, who live in the cold lands that fringe the Arctic Ocean. These are made of reindeer skins and birch bark and are easily carried when the people roam the tundra in spring with their herds of reindeer.

Like the tent, the hut has been used since the early days of home-making. Some Eskimos today still live in snow huts called igloos. In almost every part of the world wood plays an important part in house building and the lumberjacks of Canada live in houses made of logs. The people of Alpine countries live in beautiful wooden chalets, and in Burma the elephant helps man to transport the teak from which he will make homes. Bamboo huts built on stilts can still be seen in the flood regions of Thailand.

The first really great building works were produced by the ancient civilisations of Egypt and Mesopotamia, and later of Greece and Rome. These people took their art to many countries and some of their work still exists today, although most of it is in ruins.

In the Middle Ages there were many periods, or styles, in architecture, most of which began on the continent of Europe and spread to other areas.

Above **In most arctic lands there are no trees or plants to provide building materials so the Eskimos who live there have to build their homes, called igloos, out of solid blocks of snow. The Eskimos are a hardy race and find in these igloos enough protection from the winds.**

Above **A magnificent example of a 17th Century interior, the Heaven Room by Antonio Verrio c.1696 at Burghley House, England.**

Above **Nomads, being people who have no settled home and are always on the move, live in tents because they can be packed up easily when the time comes to move on. The tents in this picture are tepees and were once used by some tribes of American Red Indians.**

Above **Some of the finest castles were those built by the Crusaders. This scene, copied from a 14th-century painting, depicts the capture of Jerusalem. On the right is an archer taking aim through the window of a medieval castle.**

Below **A typical castle of the Middle Ages.**

Below **Troy was the ancient city in Asia Minor which Homer writes about in the** *Iliad.* **The archaeologist Heinrich Schliemann dug up the site in modern times and found traces of nine different cities buried one under the other, the earliest going back over 3,000 years.**

Below **A reconstruction of the ancient city of Babylon on the banks of the River Euphrates, at the height of its power about 2000 BC.**

During the 1st century AD the Roman emperor Augustus built a magnificent home and from its site on the Palatine Hill in Rome comes our word 'palace'. Kings and emperors in the ancient world were all-powerful. They built large palaces to live in, not only to please themselves but to impress ordinary people with their wealth. Today, the ruins of some of these palaces in Egypt, Babylon and Crete are enough to suggest to us what beautiful places they were.

The emperors of old China built palaces within the walls of 'forbidden' cities, which the common people were not allowed into. Both in China and Japan the emperors hid themselves away behind these walled cities and their palaces were full of mystery and not built for show. The Japanese built their palaces like their houses, with blank outside walls, looking into a central courtyard.

Palaces in the modern world, which are still in use as homes, museums or show places, date mostly from the 16th–18th centuries. They were built by the rulers of European kingdoms for just the same reasons as those in the ancient world. The monarch had to make a splendid show of his royal power, and nowhere was this more true than in France, where the palace of Versailles was built for Louis XIV. It took over a hundred years to complete this enormous collection of buildings with their surrounding parks, avenues and gardens. The most splendid palace in England, at Blenheim, near Oxford, was built by the nation as a present to its great military leader, the first Duke of Marlborough, who led his country to victory in many battles against the French in the 18th century.

the oldest pyramid is the Step Pyramid at Sakkara, which is the tomb of King Zoser. The Aztec people of Mexico also built pyramids on top of which human sacrifices to the gods took place.

The Greeks developed a style of architecture which we refer to as 'classical'. It reached its highest peak of perfection in the 5th century BC at the time of Pericles and Phidias, the Greek sculptor. The Romans inherited the Greek forms and both races were masters of the art of building temples and the remains of many can still be seen today. The most perfect of them was the Parthenon, a temple to Athena on the Acropolis at Athens. A great masterpiece of Roman architecture is the Pantheon in Rome, which was begun in 27 BC, rebuilt by the emperor Hadrian, and is still used as a church.

The houses that people have built over the centuries tell us something of the way they lived, but their churches, temples and monuments tell us even more. They tell us a little of what people thought.

In prehistoric times, centuries before Christ was born, people had many different gods. Early man did not build churches but something of his religious beliefs do show in the monuments, wall paintings and other artforms of his time. The monument at Stonehenge on Salisbury Plain in England was probably begun about 1900 BC. It is clear that Stonehenge was a very important religious centre, and served as a temple of the sun for hundreds of years. It is the largest and most impressive monument of its period in northern Europe.

The first true temples appeared much later than this with the ancient civilisations of India, China and the Near East. Because people feared the gods the temples were lavishly built so as to please them. Both private worship and public rituals took place in the temples and they were often very large. The Temple of Ammon at Karnak in Egypt, built about 1200 BC, had an inner and an outer temple, and only the king and the priests were allowed in the inner chamber.

As a place of worship this form contrasts sharply with the pyramid-shaped temples called ziggurats in Mesopotamia. Pyramids were also part of the landscape in Egypt, where

Above **Stonehenge on Salisbury Plain, England, believed to be the finest Bronze Age monument in Europe. It consists of enormous blocks of stone standing in concentric circles, although some of the stones have disappeared. Its actual function is not known but it is generally supposed to have been connected with sun worship.**

Right **The picture shows part of the magnificent temple of Rameses III who was a pharaoh of ancient Egypt. The statue is of the pharaoh himself and he is depicted as wearing the double crown of Upper and Lower Egypt. The statues in the inner court have been badly damaged since it was first built about 1200 BC.**

Below **The pyramids of ancient Egypt have inspired explorers and archaeologists for many hundreds of years because of the strange air of mystery and legend which surround them. Excavations in modern times have shown that they were built as vast tombs for the pharaohs. As the Egyptians believed in life after death, they filled the tombs with all kinds of articles which had been used and enjoyed in life.**

Left **St. Basil's Cathedral, Moscow. The Orthodox Church, of which it is a part, is found chiefly in Russia, Greece and Eastern Europe.**

Below **This modern building which is in Tel Aviv, Israel, offers a striking contrast in architectural style when compared with the others on this page.**

Left **The Taj Mahal built in 1650 at Agra in India by a Mogul emperor, Shah Jehan, as a tomb for his wife. It has a brilliant white exterior and its decorations are very rich in style.**
Below **St. Peter's Rome. As there has been a church on this site since the early days of Christianity, it is of great historic interest and houses priceless works of art.**

When Christianity came it spread quickly through the civilised world, although not many churches were built in the early years. Then the Roman Empire split up and a second capital was founded at Byzantium, a town which was renamed Constantinople and which is known nowadays as Istanbul. The style of the Byzantine church, on which domes were a prominent feature, changed little during the next 1,000 years. Probably the finest and most famous example is the church of St. Sophia in Istanbul, which is now used for worship by the Moslems and known as the Great Mosque.

During the 11th century a new way of building churches developed, called Romanesque. These churches had round arches supported by large pillars. In France in particular the churches were decorated with impressive solemn sculpture.

During the Gothic period an enormous amount of energy and money went into the building of churches. Gothic buildings had graceful pointed arches and large windows instead of thick walls. Stained glass was used in the windows for the first time.

There are many beautiful temples in the Orient, such as the Taj Mahal in India, and the exotic golden temples to Buddha in the Far East.

Thinking and believing

Below The gods of ancient Rome were the counterparts of the Greek gods. The head is that of Minerva, who was identified with Athena.

In ancient times, man knew little of the world apart from the area where he lived. He believed that spirits, who lived in rivers, trees or rocks, controlled things like darkness, sun, thunder, rain, life and death. The people thought that they must please the spirits so that the spirits would help them, and they prayed to them and offered sacrifices.

Right Zeus, the great god of the Greek family, or pantheon. The gods are remembered today by myths and legends and it is sometimes forgotten how real they were to the Greeks, whose religion was based on a passionate belief in the existence of the gods.

Below Reconstruction of the inner shrine of the Parthenon which contained the mighty statue of Athena, goddess of wisdom, made of ivory and pure gold.

Many early tribes thought that some animal, plant or other object was sacred to their tribe and had to be especially cared for. They also felt that other objects or actions had to be avoided for the safety of the tribe. These beliefs are still held in certain parts of the world, though they are now dying out.

When people began to live in villages and towns, their religions became more advanced. The people of the settlements in the river valleys of Egypt and Mesopotamia, nearly 5,000 years ago, all had their own gods, most of which they feared. These people believed that if they worshipped their gods and made sacrifices to them the gods would bring them good weather and good crops.

At this time also man began to attach a religious significance to the changing seasons and celebrate these changes. The people had priests, men

Below Jupiter, the supreme Roman god.

trained to understand the gods, who told everyone how to behave and how to worship. Shrines and temples were built to the gods.

The ancient Egyptians believed that life on earth would continue after death, so long as the dead person was helped into the next life. The bodies of their kings were mummified – spread with oil and wrapped in bandages to keep them lifelike – and put in royal tombs, or pyramids, after a long ceremony had been performed.

About 4,000 years ago, in ancient Greece, the people worshipped many gods, believed to be all-powerful beings which never died. The Greeks believed the gods to be like men and women, only taller, stronger and more beautiful. They thought of them as a

Above **When a pharaoh of ancient Egypt died his body was preserved and placed in an elaborate coffin. This is one of the splendid golden coffins in which the body of Tutankhamen was found.**

Below **A statue of a worshipper from the ancient state of Sumer.**

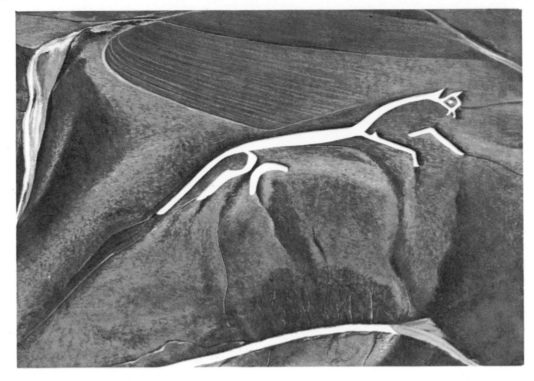

Above **The Celtic peoples in Britain cut several of these white chalk figures in hillsides. Their purpose is not known but probably they were religious in character. This white horse can still be seen at Uffington in Berkshire. The turf of the hillside is removed to reveal the chalk.**

family, or pantheon, with Zeus, the king of the gods, at the head of the family. Hera was his wife, Poseidon the god of the sea, Ares the god of war and Aphrodite the god of love.

The gods were supposed to eat special food, called ambrosia, and a special drink called nectar. The Greeks thought that if a human being could eat some of this special food he would never die. The Greeks believed they had a duty to worship the gods, and they offered them prayers and sacrifices. For the sacrifices, meat, cakes or grain were used. Some was burned on the altar, while the rest was eaten by the congregation.

The Romans, who first settled around Rome in the 8th century BC, believed in similar gods to the Greeks, but they thought that they must worship them in the right way and at the right times. If they did so, the gods would give them all they wanted. Jupiter was the king of the gods, Juno his wife, Neptune the god of the sea, Mars the god of war and Venus the god of love.

In the 14th century AD, the Aztec empire ruled in Mexico. Their religion was very cruel. They believed that to make the gods strong and powerful they must offer them human sacrifices. So the Aztecs made war with their neighbours and captured prisoners in order to kill them at religious ceremonies.

An Aztec ceremonial knife from Mexico.

Living religions

The Hebrews were the first people to believe in a supreme God, who had created the world and now controlled it. They lived in Palestine in the 19th century BC. Later they were known as Jews and their religion Judaism. The story of their early sufferings is given in the first five books of the Old Testament of the Bible. Jews believe they are the chosen people of God and that a Messiah is coming to save them. When Jesus was born, a few Jews believed he was the Messiah. After the Jews lost Jerusalem, in AD 70, they did not have their own country again until 1947 when the state of Israel was formed. There are about 10 million Jews today.

Jesus Christ was the founder of the Christian religion. His life and teachings, and the teachings of his disciples, are told in the New Testament of the Bible. When Jesus died he had few followers, but now about one-third of the human race is Christian. This is the only great religion which claims that its founder is more than a prophet. Christians believe much of the Jewish teachings, but also that Jesus is the Son of God who by his crucifixion paid for the sins of mankind, and that their present life is a preparation for life after death.

Moslems also believe in one all-powerful God, whom they call Allah. Their religion, Islam, was founded in

Below left **Buddhist monks in their traditional robes.**

Below right **A reading from the sacred book of Islam, the Koran.**

Bottom **A street in Damascus, almost unchanged for 2,000 years.**

Arabia in the 7th century AD by Mohammed. According to tradition, Mohammed received messages from God telling him to go out and teach the people that there was only one God and that he, Mohammed, was his prophet. Mohammed's sayings are written down in a book called the Koran. The Arabs conquered other countries and so the Islamic religion spread. Today there are about 200 million Moslems.

The Hindu religion is very complicated and has no one founder. It is thought to have started in India in 1500 BC. Hindus believe that when someone dies he may be reborn, and each person has a series of lives. They believe that their actions in this life

determine the sort of life they have in the next, but they seek to escape from the cycle. There are about 250 million Hindus in the world today.

Buddhism was formed in the 6th century BC in India by Gautama. Nothing of his life was written until 200 years after he died, but there are legends about him. He thought men suffered because they were full of selfish desires, and they could only escape and achieve *nirvana* (blessed peace) by training themselves not to have desires. He was called Buddha (enlightened one) by his followers. Buddism has now almost disappeared in India, but there are about 150 million Buddhists in other countries.

China and Japan have both been influenced by Buddhism, but have their own religions: Confucianism and Taoism in China, and Shinto in Japan. Confucius lived in the 6th century BC. He was concerned with the way men treat their fellows and taught ancestor-worship.

Lao Tzu, who lived 50 years before Confucius, is thought of as the founder of Taoism. He taught that men should do nothing and live in harmony with nature. Shinto followers believe the Japanese emperors are descended from the gods, and they too worship nature.

Above **A 9th-century figure of the Shinto goddess Nakatsu-Hime. She is dressed in Japanese Court dress.**

Top **8th-century temple from Mamallapurum, India.**

Above **Two Jewish boys studying the bible.**

Below **Jesus as a boy, working in his father's carpenter's shop. A painting by Millais.**

Above **The Dome of the Rock, Jerusalem. Built in 691, it is the first monumental building erected by the Moslems to have survived intact.**

Medicine and hygiene

In primitive times medicine was connected with religion. The first people to study medicine as a science were the Greeks. Hippocrates, who was born about 460 BC, was the first true doctor, and during his lifetime Greek medical knowledge spread to other parts of the world. The Romans, always great organisers, built hospitals in all their major towns.

Galen, an outstanding Greek physician who practised in Rome lived from AD 130–201. His medical theories were followed for some 1,500 years. Galen was able to distinguish between nerve, muscle and tendon, but he made the mistake of thinking that food was carried to the liver and turned into blood. For hundreds of years after Galen there was no major advance in medicine and it was left to the Moslems in the East to make new discoveries.

By the 16th century surgery was more widely practised and doctors had learned a lot about anatomy. There followed a great revival of learning with doctors torn between the Arabian and Greek schools of thought.

Between 1590 and 1640 the thermometer was invented and methods of accurately timing the pulse rate had been introduced. In 1628 an Englishman, William Harvey, published his work on the circulation of the blood, completely disproving Galen's theories. Microscopes were invented by the 17th century and the Dutchman, Anton van Leeuwenhoek, had discovered bacteria with their aid.

By the 18th century much more had been learned about the heart, respiration, and the nervous and reproductive systems. Towards the end of the century it was at last realised how

Above **Primitive people believe that sickness is caused by evil spirits which must be driven out of a patient. To do this, they call in a medicine man like the one shown here.**

Left **The Greek scientist, Hippocrates, who was the first real doctor, was born about 460 BC. Today, new doctors still sometimes take the 'Hippocratic Oath' and agree to keep the code of conduct laid down by him.**

Below **Here, Achilles, who is one of the legendary figures of ancient Greece, is seen bandaging a warrior. Achilles is supposed to have been taught the art of healing by a centaur called Chiron.**

Left **A series of medieval drawings of surgeons and their patients.**

Above **Edward Jenner (1749–1823) the discoverer of vaccination which has almost eliminated smallpox from the civilised world.**

important hygiene was and drainage and water supply systems were installed. Louis Pasteur discovered the science of immunology and the advantages of vaccination against disease.

In 1847 James Young Simpson began the use of chloroform, a substance that prevented patients from feeling pain during an operation. This revolutionised surgery, which remained dangerous until Joseph Lister discovered that the use of antiseptics stopped infection in the wounds made by surgery. Penicillin, a drug which kills bacteria, and which we call an antibiotic, was discovered by Alexander Fleming in 1928.

Since the early years of the 20th century, much has been learned about medicine and surgery. The most spectacular advance has been in the field of transplant surgery, with the first attempts at grafting new kidneys and hearts.

Right **Thanks to radiology, it is possible to see inside people. Here, a surgeon is looking at the chest of the patient in the X-ray machine.**

Below **Here blood is being taken from a donor. It will then be classified and labelled and placed in a blood bank ready to save someone's life.**

Right **The picture shows a typical scene in the operating theatre of a modern hospital. The surgeons and nurses are wearing sterile coats, caps and face masks to prevent germs infecting the patient.**

Writing and printing

Writing is a tool of a developed society and is one of the things which separates civilised man from the savage. In the old worlds of Egypt and Mesopotamia writing was a rare art, practised mostly by scribes. It was only with the successful use of printing in the 15th century that knowledge became more readily available. Very gradually, writing began to be thought of as an accomplishment for the majority of people. But even today this is still only true of western society. There are many backward and underprivileged people for whom education in the basic skills is still lacking.

Some of the earliest systems for recording events were what are called mnemonic, which means something used as an aid to memory in recalling and recording facts. The Peruvian *quippu* or knotted string is an example, as is the familiar knotted handkerchief which is supposed to remind us of some fact to be recorded or action to be performed. Notched sticks served a similar purpose in keeping records of sums of money and weights of goods.

Later systems of writing were pictorial, that is they consisted of actual picture-drawings of the event to be recorded. Ideographic systems use conventional symbols to suggest a particular idea. The numbers 1, 2, 3, 4, 5, 6, 7, 8, 9 are called ideograms and exist without being dependent on language. The ideogram '2' is interpreted as two, or *deux*, or *due*, according to the language one speaks, but in what it suggests the ideogram is international.

Phonetic systems can be verbal, in which images are used directly to suggest particular words, or syllabic, when images are used to suggest each separate sound of a word, such as 'bee' and 'leaf' = belief. Alphabetical systems break a word up into individual elements and a conventional symbol is used to signify each one.

Above **These pictures show wampum beads which were small tubular shells used by North American Indians instead of money and for record purposes. The quippu (1) was used by the ancient Peruvians as a recording device. The wampum circle (2) and belt (3) were to record events, like minutes of a council meeting.**

Below **Tally sticks, used to record numbers and as a method of keeping accounts.**

Above **This tablet, showing Ashurbanipal, the emperor of Assyria, commemorated his founding of a temple. In his palace at Nineveh, Ashurbanipal had a 'library' of such tablets, most of them telling stories of the history of the time.**

Below **This stone, found at Rosetta near the Nile, is important because it led to the deciphering of Egyptian hieroglyphics. It is written in various languages.**

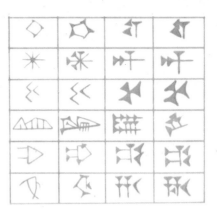

Above **Here we have an example of cuneiform writing which was in use in the Near East for a long period from about 3000 BC onwards. During its long life, it underwent some changes and was used for more than one language. True cuneiform is as shown in this picture and was written with a pointed stylus which made little wedges in the stone tablet. Today, though, the name is often used loosely for other old forms of writing.**

Above **Pictures like these are to be found painted on the walls of many ancient Egyptian tombs. The strange looking creatures are gods and behind them can be seen characters written in hieroglyphic, one of the most important ancient systems of writing. This writing consisted of various picture symbols instead of words.**

Left **This is a fragment of the Dead Sea Scrolls discovered in jars hidden in a cave in 1947. Written in Aramaic, they are an early copy of some books of the Bible. Aramaic was a Semitic language close to Hebrew and was the language spoken in New Testament times by Jesus Christ and His apostles.**

Below **Some writing instruments.**

Left **These symbols show how the Roman letter 'A' may have evolved from a picture sign for an ox (Aleph in Phoenician which became the Greek Alpha).**

Below **The Greeks sometimes wrote in both directions. This style of writing is called boustrophedon, which means 'ploughing like an ox'.**

IFYOUREADTHISWRI
TINGFIRSTFROMLEF
TTORIGHTTHENFROM
RIGHTTOLEFTDOWNT
HELINESYOUWILLTH
ENUNDERSTANDWHAT
BOUSTREPHEDONWRI
TINGREALLYISALL
ABOUT

Printing and making books

Printed books, magazines and newspapers are so much a part of our everyday life that it is difficult to imagine what it must have been like in the days before the invention of printing. When talking about the invention of printing it is necessary to know what is meant by the term 'printing'.

People in the ancient world, particularly in Mesopotamia and Egypt, were able to transfer images by the impression of seals, which worked rather like rubber stamps do today.

Left **An 18th-century printing press. The printer is taking an impression from the type.**

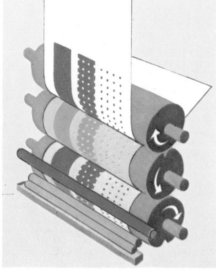

Above left **The Letterpress process. This is a method of printing from a raised surface.**

Above centre **Offset Lithography. A method of printing from a flat surface. The image on the bottom cylinder is transferred to the rubber surface of the centre cylinder. The image is finally printed on paper.**

Right **Photogravure. This is a method of printing from an incised surface. The cylinder is immersed in ink and then wiped clean. Ink remains in the incised surface of the cylinder and when pressure is applied, the paper lifts the ink out of the recesses.**

These were made of wood or clay, and were used as signatures or personal marks by traders. But this crude form of printing never developed into the more complicated craft which records the written word by some mechanical means.

The first real printers were probably the Chinese. In the library of the British Museum in London is an ancient Chinese manuscript called the Diamond Sutra, which was printed from wood blocks in AD 868. The date is known since it is inscribed on the manuscript, which is generally reckoned to be the earliest surviving printed 'book'. It is also believed that the Chinese may have begun printing as early as the 7th century AD.

The process used in these early days is called block printing, a method which continued to be employed in Europe right up to the 15th century. As a method it was costly and took a long time. In block printing, letters were written in ink, in reverse, on a smooth block of wood. Then the surface of the wood around the letters was cut away until they appeared standing out in relief. The raised letters were then inked and an impression taken.

The one idea which really speeded up printing and made possible the production of a number of copies of a single book was the invention of movable type. As it happened it was also the Chinese who thought of this first. A man named Pi-Sheng did make some wooden movable type in the 11th century, but as the Chinese language is not an alphabetical one and uses many characters, the idea was never developed.

In Germany, about 1440, Johann Gutenberg, working in Strasburg and afterwards in Mainz, invented metal moulds into which hot liquid was poured to produce separate letters. The first books printed from this movable type were published in the 1450s. The famous 42-line Bible (the

name refers to the number of lines on a page) attributed to Gutenberg appeared in 1455. After this, printing spread rapidly to other countries in Europe.

The hand printing press remained in general use for over 400 years, with few variations in its essential features. Power was first applied to printing when steam rotary machines were used to print *The Times* newspaper in London in 1814. Such machines as the Linotype and Monotype made the job of composing type easier and quicker. Rotary machines were built which could print hundreds of thousands of copies of newspapers and magazines in a few hours.

Since then the development of printing has been concerned with cheaper, faster and better methods of producing the enormous mass of printed material which the modern world demands. Automation is now the key word in printing, as it is in so many other sectors of industry.

Left **The four stages of putting a book together. Books are generally bound in 16 or 32-pages signatures. Several signatures make up the complete text. The books are then cased and bound.**

Right **Colour printing. Most modern colour reproduction is printed in four colours – yellow, cyan (blue), magenta (red) and black.**

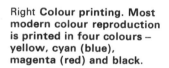

Above **Potato printing. The simplest method of relief printing.**

Right **A modern Monotype composing keyboard.**

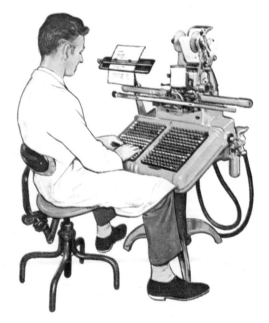

Artists and craftsmen

Primitive art

The art of early man was an expression of his feelings about life; most of all, his need to survive. The vital thing was to be successful in the search for food and, later, when man became a farmer, to grow good crops. The earliest forms of art, such as the magnificent cave paintings discovered in France and Spain, were probably a means of capturing an animal's spirit, so that it could be overcome in the hunt.

Primitive art has much to do with primitive religion. Man's fears of the natural world and his desire to control nature caused him to make such images as he thought would please the gods and spirits. In the making of these things he painted or modelled directly from his own feelings – no one taught him how to create his images. In this sense primitive art does not belong to any one period for it has always existed in men's lives and is still practised today in various parts of the world.

Above **A North American ritual mask. Most primitive people believe that the head of a person contained his spirit. Partly for this reason, masks were often used in religious ritual and magic. Some masks represented spirits of gods.**

Right **In various parts of the world, there are to be found paintings on the walls of caves and many of them date back thousands of years. They often depict wild animals like this boar.**

Below **This is a bark painting of a kangaroo hunt. Some early artists drew the animal's internal organs like this.**

Below **Because heads, and therefore masks, contained spirits, they were often used to drive away evil spirits, as in healing and fertility rites. This picture shows a dance mask from the Ivory Coast in West Africa.**

Left **Part of an embroidered mantle border from Peru dated about AD 400.**

Below **A Pueblo Indian clay vessel of the 19th century.**

Above **Aboriginal paintings found in a cave in Australia.**

Left **This Chinese sacred vessel belongs to the Shang period (14th–12th centuries BC). The man is not being devoured by the tiger. Instead, he is clinging to his 'tiger-spirit' for protection.**

Right **This strange looking object is in fact an Eskimo mask. It is made of painted wood and feathers and belongs to the 19th century.**

Below **Here is a turquoise mosaic ornament which came from Mexico and is of the 14th or 15th century.**

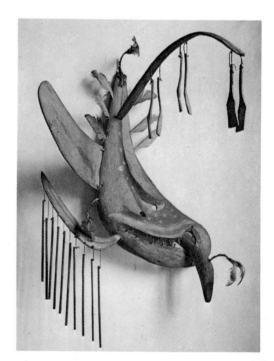

47

Art in the ancient world

The art of the ancient civilisations was already very highly developed when, on the evidence of archaeological finds, we first became aware of it. An interesting fact about the style of art, in ancient Egypt in particular, is that it changed hardly at all for hundreds of years, unlike art today.

We know about the art of the early Egyptians from the pyramids and tombs they built. Into the tomb of a dead person was put a likeness of his head, carved out of granite. On the walls of the tomb were paintings of scenes of everyday life. This was done to help the dead person travel into the next life.

Artists in those days did not look at a subject and draw what they saw. They wanted to show everything as clearly as possible and show it from the best view, even if this meant painting or carving in a stylised, formal way. It was quite usual for a drawing of a side view of the head to have on it a front view of an eye. The

Above **Ur of the Chaldees** was an ancient Sumerian city believed to be the birthplace of Abraham. Here we see two sides of a casket which is known as the 'Royal Standard' of Ur.

Above **An ancient Egyptian wall painting showing a servant bringing gifts to his master. The Egyptians believed that after death, a man could enjoy all the material things he had in life and so this idea was expressed in art.**

Right **This magnificent throne is made of wood and plated with real gold and silver. It was found in the tomb of Tutankhamen who was a relatively unimportant pharaoh of the mid-14th century BC.**

Above **This bronze Greek statue of a young man was found in fragments in the sea and then carefully reconstructed.**

Egyptians also had strict rules about style. For instance, if a sculptor made a statue of a seated figure, the figure had to have his hands on his knees.

Art in ancient Mesopotamia is less well-known to us today. One reason is that the people made no stone buildings, but used baked bricks which eventually crumbled away. Stone sculpture, too, was rare. The Mesopotamian kings built monuments to celebrate victory in war. At first these were sculptures showing the conquered king surrendering, but later they told the whole story of the war in pictures. Art in Mesopotamia is similar in style to Egyptian art, but not as formal and neat. Some of the pictures look very convincing.

On the island of Crete there were artists who worked in a much more free and graceful style than the artists either in Egypt or Mesopotamia. Their art was copied on the mainland of Greece.

Art in Greece in about 1000 BC was rather primitive. Pottery was decorated with plain geometric patterns. Buildings, probably made of wood,

Left **This is a ritual vessel carved in the shape of a bull's head. Dated about 1500 BC, it was found in the Little Palace at Knossos in Crete. The bull played a very important part in Cretan mythology as it was the emblem of 'The Great God'.**

were constructed in a simple style. But during the following centuries in Greece there was a great change in the world of art. Buildings, often beautiful temples to the gods, were built of stone, with stone columns instead of wooden props.

The Greeks found new ways of picturing the human body, drawing it in a more lifelike way. Feet had been drawn by the Egyptians as seen from the side, but the Greeks began to draw them as seen from the front. Materials changed, too, some statues being made in bronze and buildings in marble.

Greek artists had a style which was very graceful, simple and clear. People became interested in painting and sculpture because of their beauty, not just because of their religious or political meaning. Eventually Greek artists learned to draw moving people, and give faces expressions. When Alexander the Great founded the Hellenistic Empire, in the 4th century BC, art became less refined and more dramatic.

This Hellenistic style was copied by most artists until the Romans had established their huge empire by about AD 200. The Romans introduced new types of buildings, including aqueducts (which carried water across the land) and public baths. The Romans were fond of portraits, and artists made these more lifelike than ever before. Picture stories were popular, too, and the Romans liked them to be accurate – accuracy was more important to them than beauty or dramatic effect. And Roman artists learned to draw landscape pictures.

Above **This sculpture of a ram in a thicket was found at Ur.**

Left **A statue of a winged human-headed bull found at the palace of Sargon II, king of Assyria, 722–705 BC.**

Art in the western world

As the Roman Empire broke up and the Christian church became established, art began to change once again. The early Christian artists wanted their work to be as simple and clear as possible, as the Greeks had, rather than completely accurate. No statues were allowed in Christian churches, but the church in the West allowed paintings. These were simple illustrations which told stories for those who could not read. Sometimes these pictures would be mosaics of pieces of coloured glass or stone.

The city of Constantinople, at the heart of the Byzantine Empire, was relatively unaffected by the barbarian invasions of the Dark Ages. It produced some of the most nearly perfect buildings and works of art ever made. These include the church of St. Sophia in Constantinople and the mosaics of Justinian and Theodora in the Church of San Vitale, Ravenna.

The Dark Ages (between AD 500 and 1000) was a time of many wars and upheavals. Various tribes invaded Europe bringing with them their traditional crafts of wood carving and metal work. They were very skilled and made complicated patterns, sometimes of twisted bodies of dragons. In England this had an influence on Christian art, where manuscripts were illustrated with intricate patterns. Most art at this time was religious, but the Bayeux tapestry tells the story of the Norman conquest of England in 1066 in simple, clear pictures.

Above **A Byzantine mosaic in the oratory of Galla Placidia, built during the 5th century at Ravenna in Italy. It shows the Good Shepherd with His lambs.**

Above **The Book of Kells, an 8th-century illuminated manuscript of the Gospels written in Latin. This great treasure is kept in Trinity College, Dublin.**

Above **A section of the Bayeux Tapestry, a long strip of linen embroidered in wool. It depicts the conquest of England in 1066 and is now in the Bishop's palace at Bayeux in Normandy.**

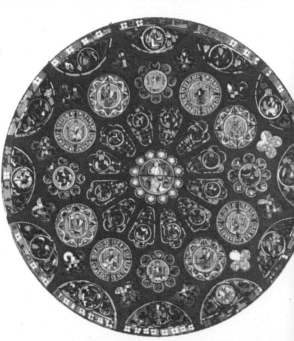

Right **One of the rose windows of medieval stained glass in the Cathedral of Notre Dame in Chartres, France. The building dates from about 1194 and is often regarded as the best example of Gothic architecture in the whole of Europe.**

At the beginning of the 11th century the most powerful influence on the development of art was still the church. Stone carving and metal work decorated the massive churches of the Romanesque period. Wall paintings, called murals, were painted, often in panels. They looked like enlarged pages from a Bible picture-book. In the monasteries manuscripts continued to be illustrated with brilliantly coloured borders and initial letters.

A hundred years later a new architectural style, called Gothic, appeared. It was light and graceful, and sculpture and painting had a Gothic style as well. Artists tried to make figures look convincing and tell a story movingly. Figures in manuscript drawings showed feelings, though the illustrations did not look lifelike, as they had to be fitted into a pattern. France was the leader of the Gothic style, which was soon copied by other countries. It was some time before its influence was felt in Italy, where artists were still influenced by the old Byzantine style.

One Italian painter however, Giotto di Bondone (1267–1337), brought a great change to art. His individual style broke away from Byzantine influence and his paintings had life— the scenes in them looked as if they were really happening. His work influenced artists in northern Europe, as Gothic art began to spread south into Italy. Among the most interesting

Below **A beautiful bird shaped brooch dating from the 6th century. It was found in Saragossa, Spain.**

Above **A carved head from a cart found in a Viking Ship dating from AD 850. It was unearthed in 1904 at Oseberg, in Norway.**

Above **The sun-chariot from Trundholm in Denmark. It was found in fragments in 1902 by a farmer when he was ploughing a field, and has since been re-assembled. It illustrates the belief of many Bronze Age people that the sun was drawn across the heavens in a chariot.**

Left **Ever since the Christian Church was founded nearly 2,000 years ago, painters and sculptors have depicted scenes from the Gospels. One of the most beautiful of the Nativity paintings is 'The Adoration of the Magi' shown here. Painted by the Limbourg brothers in the early 15th century, it shows the wise men bringing their gifts.**

works of art during the 14th century were small objects made in metal or ivory. These were full of delicate detail. At this time, too, portraits began to be painted again.

The next century saw the great period of the Renaissance in Italy, although other important developments took place in northern Europe as well. Jan van Eyck, who lived in Flanders, improved the paint artists used by adding oil to it. He was the first successful oil painter. He studied nature and made exact copies with great care and patience. He also painted many portraits, which were more realistic than ever before.

The greatest period of Italian art was in the late 15th and early 16th centuries. This was the time of the Renaissance, when there was a rebirth of interest in the arts and sciences of ancient Greece and Rome. It was also a time when artists escaped from the dark mood of the Middle Ages and found new glory in their power to create beautiful things. Leonardo da Vinci, Michelangelo, Raphael, Titian, Durer – each man a genius – and all of them lived within the space of little more than a hundred years. And they were only the men of genius: there were hundreds of lesser but still great artists working alongside them all over Europe.

Leonardo da Vinci was the 'ideal man' of the Renaissance – artist, scientist, engineer, scholar, musician – there seemed to be no skill that he did not possess. Although we have few works of his, each one is a masterpiece. His painting of a Florentine lady known as Mona Lisa is probably the best-known picture in the world. Leonardo left many notebooks containing his drawings and thoughts on a vast number of subjects. One curious thing about them is the 'mirror-

Above **Michelangelo's heroic statue of David is one of his masterpieces. Carved out of a single block of marble it stands over 16 feet high. It was commissioned by the city of Florence, where it now stands.**

Right **Some 5,000 pages of Leonardo da Vinci's note-books have been preserved. This drawing shows his model for a kind of heli-copter, and the curious mirror-image writing he used can be seen.**

Below **Two miniatures by Isaac Oliver, an English painter who lived from 1560 to 1617. He was the pupil of Nicholas Hilliard, who founded the English school of miniature painting.**

Above **A detail from one of Albrecht Durer's engravings** *Knight, Death and the Devil.*

Below **Many tapestries were made from drawings by Raphael which were called cartoons.**

writing' which Leonardo used to make his notes. He was left-handed and wrote backwards from right to left so that his words can only be read when reflected in a mirror.

Michelangelo was another great figure of the Renaissance. He lived until he was nearly 90 and in his unusually long life saw tremendous changes in the world and in the position of the artist. As a boy Michelangelo was trained in the work-shop of a master painter, learning all the tricks of the trade and how to paint a pleasing picture. But Michel-angelo was interested in greater things. He devoted his life to paintings and statues of the human figure. Michelangelo tried to give the feeling that within every block of marble he carved, there lay already a human figure, and that when he chipped away at the stone it was simply to reveal the form which lay hidden within. His most famous work was to paint scenes from the Bible on the ceiling of the Sistine Chapel in Rome.

Raphael admired the work of Michelangelo and Leonardo and learned a lot from it. Although he did not have their majestic power his paintings look as if the paint flowed from his brush without effort. He painted many beautiful frescoes (a method of painting on wet plaster) on the walls of palaces and villas. His other great

Right *Adoration of the Magi,* by the great Spanish portrait painter, Diego Velasquez (1599–1660). In 1624 he entered the court of Philip IV of Spain and painted over 100 portraits of the royal family and their courtiers.

Below **Peter Bruegel (1520–69)** painted many country scenes of peasants. This one is called *Harvesters.*

achievement was to arrange large groups of people in his paintings in a flowing way which was pleasing to the eye.

Titian was handsome and rich, and lived in great style. He became the official painter to the court at Venice and was a great portrait painter. Even so, colour remained more important to him than the subject of his paintings. He was also one of the first artists to paint natural human figures in religious paintings. Durer is famed not only for his paintings but for his illustrations in the pages of religious books. These usually took the form of woodcuts and engravings on metal.

After the Renaissance there are many great artists and many styles in the story of art. Two artists who followed a dramatic style called Mannerism in the 16th century were Tintoretto in Italy and El Greco in Spain. The best-known painter of the Baroque style in the 17th century was Rubens, who lived in Flanders but spent many years in Italy.

In England at the beginning of the 18th century William Hogarth set out to create a new kind of painting. He planned several series of story paintings. Though he earned fame and money, it was Joshua Reynolds whose style really pleased English tastes. He borrowed from the Italian masters and painted many dignified portraits.

Towards the end of the century, ideas about art were changing. A Spaniard, Francisco Goya, painted many fine portraits which won him a position at the Spanish court. But if we look closely at his stately portraits we see that Goya revealed the bad points in the characters of his subjects as well as the good.

The English poet William Blake

Above **Another artist who gave his attention to light and colour was J. M. W. Turner (1775–1851). His 'Snowstorm' illustrated here shows how he made nature more dramatic than it was in reality.**

Below **John Constable (1776–1837) was an English painter who wanted nothing to do with 'airy visions' but only to paint nature faithfully. Here is his picture of Salisbury Cathedral in England.**

Above **This is a magnificent bronze work called 'Head of Sorrow', sculpted in 1882 by Auguste Rodin, a Frenchman.**

Left **'Nypheas' by Claude Monet (1840–1926), a French artist who helped to found the Impressionist school.**

Below **Lichtenstein's 'Wham', one of the most famous examples of Pop-art.**

was a religious man who lived in a world of his own. He refused to draw from real life and concentrated on drawing his personal visions. Few people believed in Blake and it was much later before he was appreciated. Two other English painters became famous for their landscapes – J. M. W. Turner and John Constable. They had very different styles. Turner's world was full of life and he made his pictures very dramatic. Constable's aim was to paint the countryside as it really was, in the true colours of nature.

In the 19th century some artists became dissatisfied with art as it was. The great academies of art claimed to follow the tradition of the early 16th-century painter, Raphael. A group in England called themselves the pre-Raphaelites because they thought they must follow an earlier tradition, but their movement was not very successful and did not last long.

At the end of the century in France a group of artists looked at art with completely new eyes. These artists painted to give a general effect without elaborate detail. It was a long time before the Impressionists, as they became known, were accepted. Edouard Manet led the way in this movement, which included the painters Monet, Renoir and Pissarro.

One painter who was interested in the Impressionists, although he did not paint like them, was Vincent van Gogh. He was a Dutchman who went to live in the south of France in order to spend all his time painting. His pictures were full of sun and brilliant colour even when the intensity of his feelings had driven him mad. One man influenced by van Gogh in a group working in Paris at the beginning of this century was Henri Matisse. He used bright colours and his paintings were often like decorative patterns.

The 20th century has had many styles: Cubist, Abstract, Expression-

ist, Surrealist, and never before has the style of artistic expression changed so rapidly. Two famous artists of modern times are the painter Pablo Picasso, and the sculptor Henry Moore. Picasso, born in Spain, had his first exhibition when he was sixteen. At nineteen he went to Paris and studied primitive art. He led the Cubist movement but has always varied his methods, using many different and exciting styles. Henry Moore was born in Britain and is famous for his stone sculptures of human figures.

Above 'The Card Players' by Paul Cézanne (1839–1906). He was an Impressionist but his work had a more 'solid' look than that of Monet or Manet.

Below **Pablo Picasso** is one of the greatest modern painters belonging to the Cubist school. He often uses vivid colours and unusual outlines. The picture shown here is his 'The Three Dancers'.

Above **Henry Moore**, the British sculptor, has had a great influence in modern times. This picture shows his 'Mother and Child'.

Left 'The Chair' by Vincent Van Gogh, a 19th-century Dutch painter of The French Expressionist school.

55

Left crowns worn by kings and gods in ancient Egypt had a special meaning. They were considered to be magic symbols of power.

Featured in this pageant of costume through the ages are (1) Primitive man dressed in animal skins; (2) Queen from ancient Egypt; (3) Assyrian nobleman; (4) Minoan man from Crete; (5) Roman woman, 4th century AD; (6) Byzantine emperor, 10th/11th century; (7) Teutonic woman and child, c. 400–800; (8) Norman soldier at the time of the Battle of Hastings; (9) 12th-century princess; (10) Crusading knight, 12th century; (11) A king in the early 13th century; (12) Boy and girl in late 13th-century dress; (13) A lady of the 14th century; (14) Various costumes from the late Middle Ages, about 1400.

Costumes

For thousands of years clothes have been designed to suit the fashion conscious and for most of that time men's clothes have been as colourful and elaborate as women's – and, in some periods, more so. Perhaps man took a leaf out of nature's book when he discovered that male animals possessed the gayest colours and shapes.

In the days of the ancient Greeks and Romans, costumes were simple. The Greeks were great athletes who believed in the sun and air reaching their bodies, so their clothing was mostly loose robes. Women rarely wore hats except to protect them from the sun, but they did wear a great deal of jewellery. The Romans wore flowing, dignified clothes which reached to the floor, while their soldiers wore short, functional tunics.

Men rarely wore more than a ring as adornment, but women decked themselves with necklaces, bracelets, ear-rings and other elaborate jewellery. Trousers for men were not worn by civilised races until the barbarians from the East, who swooped over the Roman empire, introduced them. These trousers were similar to the ones the Cossacks wear today.

Right In the days of the Empire in ancient Rome hair-styles were elaborate, and it was not unusual for patrician ladies to keep several slaves solely for the purpose of hair-dressing. Many of the aids and devices used by women then to adorn their hair are very similar to those in use today.

In the days of the Saxons, costumes were made from linen, wool and silk and were often fur-lined. With the Saxons, as with all civilisations up to the 20th century, the dress of the nobles differed from that of the peasants in as much as their clothes were made from better materials and were generally more elaborately designed. Like the Norsemen, a Saxon noble wore trousers which were gartered from ankle to knee, a knee-length over-tunic and a cloak.

His lady wore a full-length long-sleeved kirtle over which was worn a short-sleeved tunic. The women of the time were skilful at embroidery and they used their art to decorate the tunics they wore. Saxon peasants wore clothes that were simply cut, as did the Saxon war leaders, the only addition to a warrior's costume being a chain mail shirt.

There was little change in costume in Europe until the 12th century, when new materials were brought back from the East by returning armies. These beautiful fabrics resulted in far more luxurious fashions than had been seen before. Armour had been invented and because this rusted so

quickly the surcoat was devised to cover the metal. The surcoat then became a common feature of fashion for many years. It was at this time, too, that the hood became popular. Today the hood can still be seen in the costumes of monks and friars.

Gowns and mantles were the vogue in Italy and their fashion spread north to the colder countries, where they were fur-lined to protect the wearer from the poorly heated and draughty rooms. An attractive addition to the costume of the men were gauntlets, some of which were jewelled.

The age of colour began in the 14th century and the art of blending colours became much more important in costumes. Velvets from the East were being worn and rich brocades and gleaming satins were popular. The men wore costumes which fitted their bodies more closely and, instead of the gartered or baggy trousers, tights were fashionable. Women

Above **In the 15th century a hat for women called the hennin was introduced. It consisted of a high cone made of stiff paper or linen, covered with silk. It had a long veil attached to it.**

Right **Ornaments have been worn by men and women since primitive times. The first personal decoration in this sense was the painting of the body, which is still practised by certain tribes. This had a religious or social meaning, as did the first jewellery to be made. This consisted of everyday objects which lay to hand, but man soon began to use precious metals and gems. The jewellery shown here all belongs to the Middle Ages, when very beautiful work was done.**

Above **These soldiers are wearing helmets and body armour belonging to the late 16th century.**

Below **Elaborate starched neck-dresses were popular with court ladies during the late 16th century.**

in the 14th century still tended to wear the fashions of their predecessors, although hair, which had usually been kept hidden, was now displayed. In England in 1363 a law was passed in an attempt to control personal spending. Common folk were permitted to wear only woollens, and if they were ever seen wearing the richer clothes reserved for knights and their ladies, the garments were confiscated.

In the 15th century women were once again wearing hats, but now these were very ornate constructions, sometimes copying the architectural features of buildings, such as the steeple of a church. Fighting men continued to wear suits of armour but the invention of the gun during the 14th century meant that armour

no longer protected the wearer and gradually its use died out.

During the 16th century men's costumes became more and more complicated and colourful, while women's dresses were more and more uncomfortable. For centuries they had endured awkward skirts, and by this time they were wearing vast, hooped skirts, often supported by a wooden frame.

In the 17th century the ladies of Venice were wearing enormously high heels, while women in China had their feet bound to prevent them growing. By the 18th century corsets were part of a woman's apparel. Waists became smaller and smaller as the corsets were laced ever tighter. In the 18th century, too, soldiers were wearing very showy uniforms with high-cut boots and tall hats, quite unsuitable for fighting in.

Early in the 19th century there was a marked change in European fashion and very simple designs became popular. As these tended to suit only the youngest figures, the crinoline, and later, the bustle, appealed to many more women. Men's clothes showed

On these pages are seen costumes dating from the 16th century until the 1890s. (1) 16th-century boy of noble family; (2) 16th-century peasants; (3) Man in a short open gown, and a woman, both 1540; (4) Child in mid-17th century; (5) 17th-century lady; (6) 17th-century cavalier; (7) Puritan man and woman about 1640; (8) 18th-century night watchman; (9) 18th-century nursemaid with two children; (10) Lady's walking costume; (11) Hussar and a guardsman of the 19th century; (12) Lady's evening gown, 1875; (13) Man's casual dress, 1880s; (14) Man in a frock coat and woman in walking dress of the 1890s.

Right The man is wearing a cravat and top hat of the late 18th century. Also shown are a fan (c. 1900), and a 17th-century shoe and a handbag of about 1870.

little of their former glory and became very plain.

In the 20th century women began to revolt against awkward and uncomfortable fashion, helped by such people as the American dancer, Isadora Duncan, who believed in loose, flowing clothes which allowed her dancers to move freely. For years, men's clothing has been very sober and the only fashion changes have been small alterations to such things as the width of lapels on jackets, or whether or not trousers should have turn-ups. But recently there has been a revival of interest in men's fashion and it is beginning to show signs of recapturing its variety and colour.

The beauty of past fashions can still be seen in traditional costumes, such as the elegant kimonos of Japan and the graceful saris of India. Sometimes, traditional costume reveals something of the character of its people, such as the practical national dress of the Dutch, or the dramatic frills and flounces of Spanish flamenco dancers.

Entertainment
Musicians and their music

Music was one of the first things in human life. Every primitive people possessed a form of music-making, however simple or crude. The human voice was the first musical instrument and man has always expressed his feelings with his voice as a matter of instinct. Often it was used in ceremonies to please the gods so that the hunt for food or the growing of crops would be successful.

It is not possible to say when music became an art, that is the moment when a conscious effort was first made to reproduce sounds which had previously come naturally. We know from the pictures drawn by artists in the ancient worlds of Egypt and Assyria that music played an important part in their lives. For the Egyptians in particular music performed a religious function and had a very serious purpose.

The Greeks used music in their drama, and in fact the plays of the early Greek dramatists, such as Aeschylus and Sophocles, were more like operas. The voice was used as an instrument, particularly in chorus, for declaiming the lines of a play. Although no complete piece of Greek music survives to this day, many books were written as long ago as 300 BC on subjects like harmony and musical notation (that is, the way the notes are written down).

In the Middle Ages, music, in common with most forms of art and knowledge, developed within the church, particularly the form of chanting known as Gregorian, which is still used in services today. In the 11th century an effort was made to improve on the system of notation inherited from the Greeks, and about this time Guido of Arezzo first made use of the lines and spaces which were to become the modern stave. Part singing was introduced, so that instead of always singing in unison men were able to sing different parts within one song. One of the greatest names in the history of early music is Giovanni Palestrina (1515–94) who composed music for the Mass which is still used as a model of church music today.

The first secular music, that is music which was not composed for religious ceremonies, grew up in the Middle Ages with the minstrels. These wandering vagabonds earned their living by singing and playing for the amusement of anyone who would give them a supper in return for a song. After the minstrels came the troubadours, who were often men of noble birth and were treated with honour and respect.

Above **A lute. This stringed instrument, popular in Europe in the 16th and 17th centuries, came originally from the Arab world.**

Below **Here are a rebec, a lute and a psaltery. Psalteries are a medieval kind of zither played with a plectrum.**

Bottom **This Bolivian Indian is blowing into a conch shell. Since earliest times man has used this type of shell as an instrument and it produces a loud sound rather like a trumpet.**

Left **Ancient Egypt was a highly cultured civilisation with a great love of music. Many of their wall paintings like these show they used stringed instruments.**

Here are some musical instruments from other lands. The sitar (1) is an Indian stringed instrument. Harps of various kinds and shapes (2) are to be found in most parts of the world. Figure (3) shows ceremonial trumpeters in Uganda. The peasant musician (4) from Ecuador is playing the pan pipes. The Japanese woman (5) plucks the koto. Drums and flutes are usually used to accompany it.

Left **Ludwig van Beethoven,** was a great German composer. Born in 1770, with Haydn and Mozart, he represents the Viennese classical school of composing. When he was 30, he had ear trouble and became totally deaf. This dreadful handicap did not stop him from composing many masterpieces.

Below A scene from *Les Sylphides,* a romantic ballet.

Opera, which combines acting and singing, began in the 16th century. Some Italian poets and musicians had the idea of setting certain Greek stories to music and performing them on a stage. At first, the dramatic action was much more important than the singing. Monteverdi's operas, composed in the first half of the 17th century, in which the music came first, were the first true operas. Monteverdi was also one of the first composers to employ an orchestra.

The man who did more than any other to establish the shape of the modern orchestra and to develop the symphony as the chief form of musical expression was Haydn. He lived in Vienna in the 18th century when that city was the centre of the musical world. Mozart, Beethoven and Schubert all lived in Vienna during a period when the greatest classical music was written. The romantic music of Brahms, Schumann and Chopin, and the grand operas of Wagner and Verdi, led to the new musical sounds of the 20th century.

Although modern musical instruments have become complex and often difficult to play, each of the three great classes into which they fall – percussion, wind and stringed – could be found readily to hand by primitive man.

Dancing round the world

People have always danced to express their feelings and different races have their own special dances which show something of their character. When primitive peoples danced, they often imitated animals or went through the actions of their work. By doing this they thought they were pleasing their gods. When these pagan beliefs died out, people carried on dancing for pleasure although they may have forgotten the original purpose of it. With the passing of time, some of these simple dances have undergone great changes and now need much more skill in performance.

Almost every country has its own national dances and these are performed on special or ceremonial occasions. In Finland dancers still imitate bears and seals, and in the forest

Below **The American dancer, Isadora Duncan, who died in 1927. She wore flowing draperies and danced in her bare feet. Everywhere she went she was a sensation and she had a very great effect upon the Russian ballet.**

regions many wood-cutting dances survive. In Italy and Portugal dances can illustrate the gathering of grapes for wine-making. The people of India, Japan and China perform dances with little body movement and instead use mainly the hands and arms. Even the smallest gesture has some meaning and although most of the dances are religious in origin, there are also charming dances which tell stories of birds, bees and flowers.

Countries with strong warlike traditions have dances which reflect their warriors' deeds. Yugoslavia has its own special sword dance, and the same kind of dances performed by Highlanders in Scotland are almost certainly war dances from that country's past. The Red Indians of North America have their own tribal dances, as do the many tribes of Africa.

With the increasing attractions of town life and more varied forms of entertainment, folk dancing lost a lot of its appeal but did not die out completely. People in towns adapted the dances so they could be performed in

Above **A scene from the popular classical ballet, *The Sleeping Beauty,* first produced in 1890 with music by Tchaikovsky.**

Below **Classical Indian dance is very graceful and once had close connections with Indian mythology and religion.**

ballrooms and so fit in with the new, more formal, way of life. The waltzes, quick-steps, rumbas, tangoes and fox-trots of the modern ballroom all come from the many folk dances of Europe, America and Africa.

Ballet is a form of dancing that knows no language barriers. It expresses feelings which can be understood by all who watch it. It began in the royal courts of Italy and then moved to France, where Louis XIV was himself a fine dancer. Louis founded a school of dancing in 1661, the Royal Academy of the Dance, which is still the most famous ballet

Below **When the Moors were settling in Spain up to the 16th century, they brought their traditional dances with them. These form the basis of flamenco dancing which we know in Spain today. However, the jumping, beating of the feet and the use of castanets are European in origin and were added to the Moorish dance.**

Above **Primitive African dances were once used in war or religion or in healing. Many of them have now been adapted into an exciting stage spectacle presented by the West African Ballet.**

Left **Two male dancers of the Russian Kirov Ballet. One demonstrates a classical pose in the Blue Bird solo from *The Sleeping Beauty* and the other is performing a Polovtsian dance from Prince Igor.**

school in France. Here, Beauchamps, the king's dancing master, laid down the rules of classical ballet and that is why ballet terms today are always written in French.

At the end of the 17th century ballet moved into the theatre and new schools sprang up in all the major European cities. Most of the difficult and brilliant dance steps were done by men, for women were restricted by the fashions of the time. La Camargo, a famous ballerina in the early 18th century changed women's role in ballet. She shocked Paris in 1724 by shortening her skirt and showing her ankles in order to execute more ambitious jumps and movements.

Ballet moved to Russia and it was a Russian, Sergei Diaghilev, who gave us ballet as we know it today, by deciding that music, scenery and dancing must be made to fit the story. His ballet company caused a sensation in Paris in 1909 and set the standard for all modern ballet.

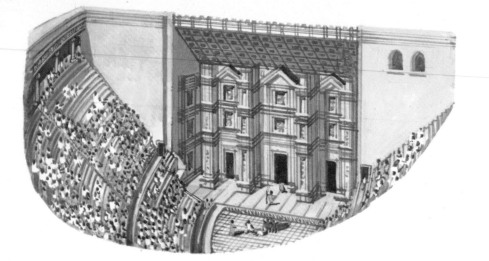

The theatre

Drama grew out of religious festivals and dances. The Greeks of nearly 3,000 years ago were the first to make these dramatic and the first to write plays and build theatres in which to act them. At first dances were performed on a dance floor on a hillside, so people could see. Then the Greeks built amphitheatres with seats cut into the hill in a semicircle. Gradually theatres developed from this.

A 'skene' or small building was built behind the central floor for the actors to wait in, then the stage was raised off the ground and a 'proskene' was built between the 'skene' and the stage. The 'proskene' consisted of columns and doors for the actors to enter and exit through.

Eventually Sophocles, one of the three great Greek writers of tragedies, that is, moving plays with unhappy endings, introduced stage scenery. He wrote at least 120 plays but we have only seven of them today. His three plays about Oedipus are probably the best known. The other two tragic writers were Aeschylus and Euripides. Another Greek playwright, Aristophanes, is famous for writing comedies – plays with happy endings. These four playwrights lived around the 4th and 5th centuries BC.

When the Romans built their theatres they did not use open hillsides but arranged the seats in tiers inside buildings. They built the first covered theatres. The Romans liked plays of action, farces and pantomimes. Roman actors wore masks, and classical actors wore shoes with very high heels.

After the fall of Rome, during the period of the Dark Ages in Europe, which lasted from about the 5th to the 11th centuries AD, theatres were pulled down and the stones used for building. The only drama was provided by troupes of minstrels, jugglers and acrobats who travelled to castles giving performances to the feudal lords. In France troubadours travelled round the country singing love songs and telling legends.

Above **By the end of the 16th century, commedia dell'arte comedies were played all over Europe. The characters, like Harlequin and Columbine, had to dance, sing and play the fool. They often wore masks.**

Right **The traditional theatre of Japan was the Noh drama and it has not changed since the 17th century.**

Far right **An actor in Kabuki costume. This traditional form of popular theatre evolved from the Noh drama.**

Above and right **In Noh drama, the actors wear masks symbolizing the type of character they are playing.**

Fairs, circuses and puppets

The fairs of long ago were not like the fairs we know today. They began as markets where foreign goods could be purchased. Fairs were usually held once a year on special saints' days which were holidays for the local people. The word 'fair' comes from the Latin word *feria*, meaning a holiday. No prices were marked on the goods as it was the custom for the seller and buyer to barter until they had fixed a price between them.

During the Middle Ages people used to come to the fairs to be amused and there were many entertainers in the crowd. Jugglers and acrobats kept the people enthralled by their daring acts, while the minstrels' songs could be heard all around. There were other entertainers with dancing bears and performing monkeys.

As time went on the buying and selling of goods became less important and the fairs became chiefly places of entertainment. The most popular part of them was the travelling theatre.

In the early 1800s the first merry-go-rounds were seen, which led to the many mechanical fun-makers of today. Fairs are now so popular that permanent ones have been built in holiday resorts.

Left **This is part of an eastern bazaar. Such bazaars date back thousands of years. Although they are so old they have changed very little over the centuries. In remote desert regions a system of barter is used — that is to say, things are exchanged for goods of the same value. In an eastern bazaar, you would be able to buy perfumes, spices, silks, meat, cooking pots and even drinking water.**

Below **Medieval fairs were not only places where people bought things but also where they could meet and enjoy themselves. Gradually, buying and selling became less and less important and fairs were more places of entertainment than anything else. At the fairs, the people could watch the jugglers, acrobats, dancers and minstrels.**

Above **The ancient Greeks first developed the art of wrestling.**

Below **Fairs today have more mechanical diversions like switchbacks and dodgem cars.**

Above **The game of table tennis is comparatively new as it was invented only at the beginning of the present century.**

Above **Chess is a very ancient board game requiring thought and skill but many children can play it quite well.**

Above **Dominoes probably came from 18th-century Italy.**

Below **Playing cards may have originated in the East but many of the games are modern.**

Above **The ancient Greeks, it is said, played billiards in the 5th century BC. These boys are playing on a quarter-sized billiard table.**

Below **This game of five stones is called by many names and has been played in one form or another throughout history.**

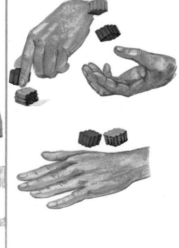

Games and recreations

Some indoor games have a long history and have been played for many years. Chess is perhaps the most important international game. It probably began in the East and spread into Europe during the time of the great Arab conquests in the 8th century. The modern game came into being in the 15th century, and one of the earliest known books about chess was printed in London by William Caxton.

Draughts have been known in Europe since the 16th century, although very similar games were played in the ancient world. Dominoes probably originated in Italy in the 18th century and the game has become very popular in cafés in France and Belgium.

Many other board games are very ancient and this type of game is probably the oldest of all. Very simple forms of them may have been played by primitive man on a 'board' scratched out on the surface of the earth or sand, with stones as counters. Some board games are played with dice, which were used in ancient times in exactly the same way as today.

Above **Swimming** is a natural activity which became a competitive sport in the 19th century. The best swimmers come from Russia, the United States and Australia.

Below **Association football** is the most widely played game in the world and attracts more spectators than any other. It began in England and is now played in every part of the globe.

Above **Although competitive skiing** dates from the end of the 19th century, skis themselves are believed to be over 5,000 years old. In fact, there is evidence from carvings that skis were used in Stone Age times.

Below left **Golf** is a very old game played originally in Scotland. The Royal and Ancient Club at St. Andrews was founded in 1754.

Below **The Queensbury Rules** under which boxing is fought were drawn up in 1867. Before this bouts were fought for prize-money with bare knuckles and often with no limit to the number of rounds.

Above **The first motor race** took place in 1894 and was run from Paris to Rouen. Grand Prix racing is now a spectacular sport and motor rallying is a useful trial ground for the motor industry.

Above **Horse racing** goes back to the time of ancient Rome. The oldest racecourse still in use is the Roodee at Chester in England, which opened in 1540.

Toys

The study of toys can tell us a great deal about the simple domestic life of people long ago. For toys reflect the larger adult world, and over the years the whole progress of man's social life is reproduced in miniature.

There have probably been toys since man first settled as a family unit in some primitive home. A kitten does not need instruction in how to chase a piece of paper for its amusement, and a primitive child played with whatever it could find as naturally as a child would today. Primitive toys have not survived simply because they

Right **These Victorian dolls' houses reflect an age of comfort when houses were much larger than they are today. The rocking horse (below) was another popular toy.**

were, most likely, natural objects and not manufactured as toys.

One of the first toys that a child plays with is a rattle, and rattles made from clay and earthenware have been found that date back to 1360 BC. In the ancient civilisations of Egypt and the Middle East there were dolls, some with movable arms and legs, although it is possible that these were sometimes made as religious effigies. There were certainly toy animals and some of these were jointed so that mouths could be made to open and shut, and tails to wag.

Many toys have survived from the classical world of ancient Greece and

Rome – dolls, balls, animals, tops – and wall paintings show the popularity of games played on a board with counters and such universal pastimes as knucklebones. It is probable that games of chance or skill were invented before toys but these were mainly for the amusement of adults. Nevertheless, it is from these games that such things as knucklebones, or five-stones, and draughts, and 'ducks and drakes' have evolved.

Very little is known of the playthings of children between the earliest civilisations and the Middle Ages. Girls played with dolls as they have continued to do ever since, and toy soldiers were made from glazed stoneware or clay and dressed in the costume of the times.

In the 16th century, hobby-horses, hoops, marbles, pop-guns, stilts and money boxes were all popular toys. The earliest-known dolls' houses date from the 17th century and originated in Germany. These dolls' houses were very large and elaborately equipped with furniture, replicas of the homes in which they were kept.

In the 18th century jigsaw puzzles were invented and the rocking horse galloped into popularity. Towards the end of the century, mechanical toys began to appear, powered by water, steam or quicksilver.

The 19th century was an era of learning and discovery and this was reflected in the toys. There were kaleidoscopes, stereoscopes and zoetropes, all toys which gave the illusion of depth and movement to flat images, and magic lanterns showing the wonders of nature. Magnetic toys were introduced early in the century, as were bubble pipes and, later on, inflatable and rubber toys.

These were days of luxury for dolls and their outfits ranged from corsets to kid gloves. Toy theatres, with 'penny plain, tuppence coloured' cut-out characters and scenery, were popular. The making of needlework samplers was a common occupation for girls.

Modern toys are often expensive, exact replicas of the real thing. Train sets, racing cars and washing machines – powered by electricity – have perhaps taken some of the fun out of make believe.

Above **The zoetrope was a device invented in the 19th century in which a series of stationary figures was given the impression of movement when the viewer looked through the slits of a revolving drum.**

Cinema

Men have always tried to communicate with each other by the use of pictures, but only in the last century have there been serious attempts to make them move. In 1824 an English doctor, Peter Roget, discovered by chance the scientific fact that a picture remains on the retina for slightly longer than it takes the eye to record it. In other words, each successive picture we see lingers a little so that one overlaps the next.

Dr. Roget's thoughts and those of a Belgian professor called Plateau, did result in the invention of toys which demonstrated this 'persistence of vision'. A typical example is the thaumatrope, which is a simple device made from a circular piece of card, on one side of which may be shown a bird and on the other its cage. By rotating the card quickly by means of pieces of string attached to its sides, the two images appear to merge and the bird is 'seen' sitting in its cage.

There were many pioneers in the early days of cinema and no one man can be credited with the major part in the invention of moving pictures. In Britain it was Robert Paul, an amateur inventor, and William Friese-Greene, a professional photographer, who led the way. In France it was

Jules Marey who studied the science of cinematography, and the Lumière brothers who developed the film as a commercial entertainment. In America Thomas Edison and his assistant W. K. L. Dickson built a motion-picture camera for roll film. All these men worked independently of each other until finally in each of their countries public performances were held.

These first moving pictures were silent and very short and there was no great public enthusiasm for them at first. It was not until pictures began to tell a story that people really became interested. In 1903 an American, Edwin S. Porter completely broke away from the old style and made *The Great Train Robbery*, the first American story film and, incidentally, the first western.

Film-making was just getting under way in Europe when the First World War broke out. This meant that the United States, who did not enter the war until 1917, were able to take the lead in supplying films to a now eager world market. The great English comedian Charlie Chaplin made his name as a 'star' in America, and directors like D. W. Griffith and Cecil B. de Mille made films which pleased the public and were the first big box-

Left **The names of some of the great stars and films are illustrated in these drawings. (1) A scene from** *The Great Train Robbery,* **the first western; (2) Charlie Chaplin; (3) Greta Garbo; (4) Humphrey Bogart; (5) Mickey Mouse; (6) Clark Gable; (7) A scene from** *Gone with the Wind;* **(8) Elizabeth Taylor; (9) Marlon Brando; (10) John Wayne; (11) Paul Newman; (12) Julie Christie; (13) A scene from** *2001, A Space Odyssey.*

Above **Filming on location for a big epic picture is an expensive business and involves hundreds of people.**

office 'hits'. The great heroes and heroines of the silver screen at that time were led by such names as Rudolph Valentino, Douglas Fairbanks and Mary Pickford.

The coming of sound made a big difference to films. After long years of experiment Al Jolson's two films *The Jazz Singer* (1927) and *The Singing Fool* (1928) saw the arrival of talking pictures. Now that actors and actresses could talk the action of a story became more human, and people responded to the appeal of the movies by filling cinemas in their millions in the 20s and 30s.

Hollywood in the United States became the world centre of film-making. In 1926 the first successful colour film, *The Black Pirate,* starring Douglas Fairbanks, was made. Then in 1929 and 1930, many spectacular musical films like *The Vagabond King* and *The Desert Song* were made. Europe came firmly back into the movie business in the 1930s with directors like Hitchcock, Korda, Clair and Pabst.

Films today have developed from one-minute peep-shows into a splendid art form, and despite the advent of television continue to entertain us.

Right **A western 'ghost' town in the United States. A permanent set such as this serves as the background for many film and television westerns. In the centre of the page is seen a projection room in a modern cinema. As each reel of film is finished the picture is switched automatically from one projector to another.**

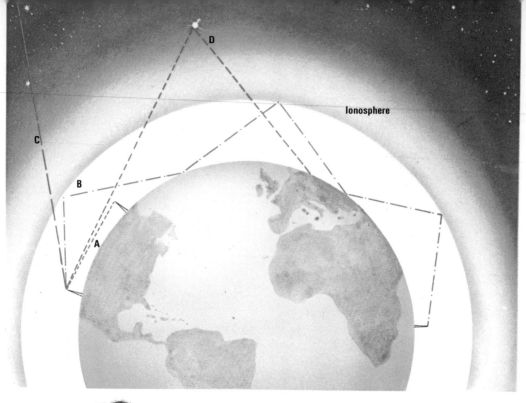

Right *Propagation of Radio Waves.*
A. Ground waves following the curvature of the earth for a relatively short distance.
B. Sky waves reflected from the ionosphere, over 80 kilometres high, and sent back to earth. Several bounces are possible and the radio signals may be sent all the way around the world.
C. Sky wave passing straight through the ionized layer. It may continue out into space, getting weaker and weaker, or be reflected back to earth by a special communications satellite.
D. A communications satellite reflects radio waves that pass through the ionosphere back to earth.

Right **Heinrich Hertz,** a German physicist who was born in 1857 and died in 1894, demonstrated the existence of radio waves in 1886. He found that radio waves behave much the same as light waves. Hertz played an important part in laying the groundwork for the invention of wireless telegraphy.

Far right **The Morse Code** and an early type of Morse telegraph system. The transmitter was powered by a battery and the signal was passed on by land lines. At the receiver, the signal was automatically punched out on tape.

Below **Guglielmo Marconi,** an Italian electrical engineer who was born in 1874 and died in 1937, invented wireless telegraphy in 1895. He came to England in 1896 and succeeded in transmitting a wireless signal for a distance of nine miles. In 1901 he was able to send a wireless signal (the letter S in Morse Code) across the Atlantic, from Cornwall to Newfoundland. He was awarded the Nobel prize for physics in 1909.

Hertz

Radio

Every hour of every day all over the earth there are millions of radio waves travelling through the air at the speed of light – 300 000 000 metres per second (or 186 000 miles per second). In order to hear them we must have a radio set, which changes the electric signals picked up by the receiving aerial into sounds that we can hear through a loudspeaker. These radio waves can be transmitted on many differ-

A ·—	G ——·	M ——
B —···	H ····	N —·
C —·—·	I ··	O ———
D —··	J ·———	P ·——·
E ·	K —·—	Q ——·—
F ··—·	L ·—··	R ·—·

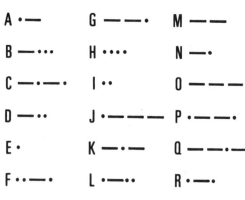

Marconi

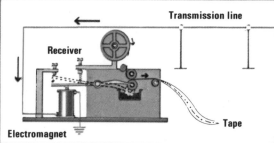

Transmission line
Receiver
Electromagnet
Tape

ent frequencies or wavelengths.

Music and voice were not the first to be transmitted by radio. Before the invention of the *microphone* (which changes sound waves into electrical waves) and the *electronic valve*, radio transmissions were all just a series of dots and dashes representing in Morse Code the letters of the alphabet.

There are two types of radio waves. The *ground wave* can follow the curvature of the earth for a short distance of about 350 km. Ground waves cannot therefore be used for transmitting radio waves between distant countries or even between cities separated by a large distance in the same country. Radio waves can be made to travel much greater distances, however, by being bounced off an electrically-charged layer in the atmosphere. This layer, called the *ionosphere*, is over 80 km above the ground. The reflected radio waves are called *sky waves*.

When short-wave radio waves are transmitted, they are reflected off the ionosphere, and can be received by radio sets many hundreds of kilometres from the transmitting set. These waves can then bounce back to the ionosphere and be reflected back to earth over and over again in a series of bounces or *skips*. This is how a radio signal from London is able to be heard in Australia, for example, thousands of kilometres away.

Not all sky waves are reflected by the ionosphere. Some high-frequency waves (short wavelengths) pass through the ionosphere into outer space. When short wave radio waves are being transmitted over a great distance they have to be reflected back to earth artificially by a *communications satellite*. When a television programme is broadcast over a great distance, a communications satellite is used to reflect the high-frequency waves.

If the ionosphere reflected every wavelength, it would be impossible to talk by radio to astronauts who have flown beyond it. There would be no field of radioastronomy if the radio waves from distant stars were unable to pass through the earth's atmosphere.

Radio is important not only in giving us information, music, and other forms of entertainment as in broadcasting, but is extremely useful for *two-way* communications between aeroplanes and control towers, and for ship-to-shore links.

Above **The Post Office Tower in Central London is used for mounting radio and TV aerials. A high tower is a good place for aerials as they transmit ground waves much further than those mounted at ground level.**

Left **A simple radio receiver. The signal from the transmitting station is picked up by the receiving aerial and is tuned in by the circuit containing the variable capacitor and coil. The signal then passes through the diode which *detects* or *demodulates* the signal so that it can be heard in the earphones.**

S ···	W ·———
T —	X —··—
U ··—	Y —·——
V ···—	Z ——··
.	·—·—·—
,	——··——
?	··——··

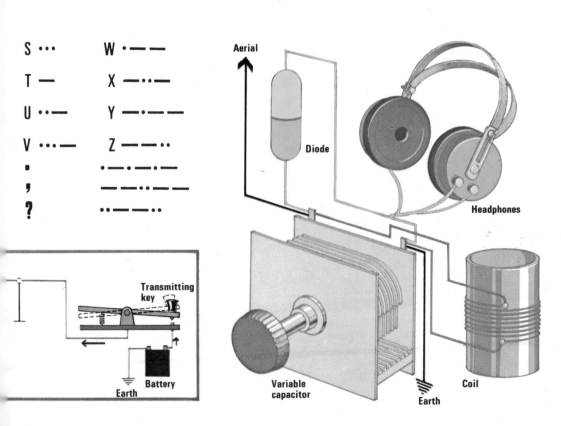

Aerial

Diode

Headphones

Transmitting key

Earth Battery

Variable capacitor

Earth

Coil

Left **John Logie Baird** was born in 1888 and died in 1946. When ill health prevented him from working as an electrical engineer he turned to studying television. He produced the first practical system. His system was used for a short while but then better ways of televising were found. His system used infrared rays.

Below The picture tube, or cathode-ray tube, consists of an electron gun which produces the electron beam and a number of magnetic coils for focusing the beam and making it scan the screen. The screen is coated with a fluorescent substance that emits light when struck by the electron beam.

Baird

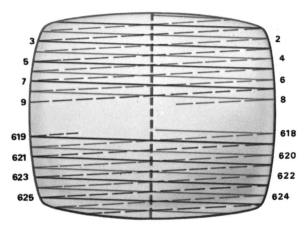

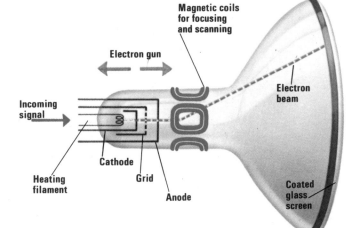

Magnetic coils for focusing and scanning

Electron gun

Incoming signal

Electron beam

Heating filament

Cathode

Grid

Anode

Coated glass screen

Above The electron beam of a black-and-white set scans the screen in a zig-zag. Each frame consists of 625 lines and 30 frames are formed in one second. The lines are at a slight angle because the beam moves steadily down the screen. Each frame is built up by first scanning the odd-numbered lines (shown black) and then the even-numbered lines (red).

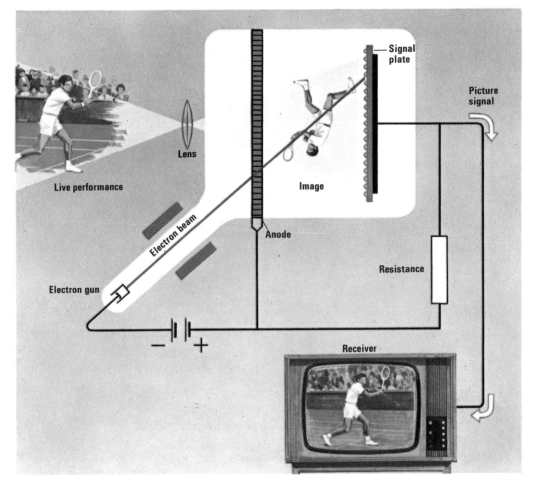

Live performance

Lens

Electron beam

Electron gun

Anode

Image

Signal plate

Picture signal

Resistance

Receiver

Television

Television shows still pictures. The pictures appear to move because they are shown one after the other at high speed. To give this impression there must be thirty pictures per second.

Each picture is divided into a number of *lines* (625 on newer sets and 405 on older sets). Each line contains several thousand bits of light or dark. To make a good picture the lines are separated into tiny bits – as many as 200 000 bits altogether. The television camera contains a signal plate covered with photosensitive dots (dots of a chemical that are sensitive to light). Each dot corresponds to one of the 200 000 tiny bits. An electron beam crosses the plate line by line and transmits the signals picked up from the dots. These are amplified and then transmitted. In the television set in your home the signals are received, amplified, and shown on the picture tube (or cathode-ray tube). In the cathode-ray tube, another electron beam is produced. This beam is made to cross the screen 625 times, so making the 625 lines. At the end of each line the beam flies back and starts the next line. These 625 lines are produced in $\frac{1}{30}$ second and each set of 625 lines is called a *frame*. As the beam crosses the back of the picture screen it gets weaker and stronger in accordance with the signals transmitted (that is, in accordance with the strength of the signals picked up from the photosensitive dots in the camera). The tube contains a special fluorescent screen, coated with chemicals, which glow under the impact of the electron beam. The stronger the beam, the brighter the light. The set also contains a loudspeaker for producing the sound and a synchronizing system for keeping the sound and picture together.

Colour television is more complicated. There are three electron beams each of which carries the signal for one of the colours, red, blue, and green. The screen of the picture tube is coated with $1\frac{1}{4}$ million tiny dots of phosphor, arranged in groups of three. A phosphor is a substance that emits light when an electron beam falls on it; each of the three phosphors used emits only one of the three colours red, blue, and green. So the blue phosphor emits blue light when the electron beam carrying the blue signal falls on it, and so on. These three colours can be combined in different proportions to give all the other colours of the original televised scene.

Television can be either broadcast, as it is for entertainment, or it can be transmitted by wire. This is called *closed-circuit television*. Closed-circuit television is used for a number of purposes. For example, it can be used in hospitals to enable students to see the details of an operation.

Science

Time, counting and measuring

It was the ancient Egyptians who invented a way of registering the passing of time at night or when the sun was not visible. This was the water clock, in which the level of water in a vessel was gradually lowered over a marked time scale by the controlled leaking away of the liquid through a hole. The Greeks had a more complicated form of water clock, called a clepsydra, and there were other 'clocks' in the ancient world based on the burning down of marked candles or knotted ropes.

In the Middle Ages there were sundials, and hour glasses in which sand slowly trickled from top to bottom of a glass vessel through a narrow neck.

Here are some ancient methods of telling the time. The hour-glass (1) works like an egg timer. A similar principle is used in the water bowl (2) which is emptied through a drip hole. The knotted string (3) is burnt like a fuse. Each time the smouldering end reaches a knot, it marks the passage of an hour. The sundial (4) shows the time by shadows cast by the sun. The lantern clock (5) is of the 18th century and (6) is a modern electric clock.

Below **Before** land can be developed for building or be excavated by archaeologists, it has to be surveyed by means of survey tapes, levels, a prismatic compass and a theodolite. The picture shows a surveyor using a theodolite.

These have survived in the old-fashioned egg-timers still used today. The first clocks were made in the 14th century, and there is one at Salisbury Cathedral in England, still in working order, which is said to be the oldest clock in the world.

Registering the passing of time is not only important in everyday life, it is also vital for such things as the navigation of ships. At first, sailors used the position of stars in the sky to help them decide their course and location at sea. But it was essential to know the time. This is why an especially accurate clock called a chronometer was invented. The first successful one was built by John Harrison in the 18th century. Accuracy in a clock has always been important, and today there are atomic clocks using the movement of electrons as a standard of time measurement which are estimated to lose or gain as little as one second in every 6,000 years.

Two of the first scientific inventions were a means of recording facts and the ability to make measurements.

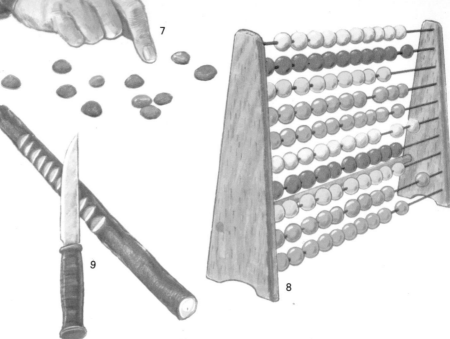

Above **When early man learnt to count, he did so by means of small pebbles (7) and later he used beads on a frame (8) for the same purpose. Tally sticks (9) were used when people did a business deal. The amounts were notched on a stick which was then split down its length, each man taking one as a record.**

Below **In coastal navigation, a line is charted showing the route to be taken. Another line drawn through the compass points on the chart, gives the compass bearing by which to steer.**

The earliest ways of recording facts was to knot string and notch wooden sticks.

It was natural for early man to use his fingers, thumbs and toes to calculate. Counting in tens and scores (twenties) has an obvious origin in the fact that we have ten fingers on our hands and ten toes on our feet. The old Roman numerals I, II, III etc., may be related to visual signs that can be made with the fingers and thumbs – one finger, two fingers, three fingers and so on. The very word 'calculate' comes from the Latin *calculus*, meaning a pebble, or little stone, and this is a link with early reckoning by means of seeds, counters or pebbles.

The numbers 1 to 9 in the system used today in the western world probably came from ancient India, although they are known as Arabic numerals. These numerals, which had been used by the Arabs for many years, were taken over by the people of Europe in the Middle Ages in place of Roman figures. The 0 or zero was added later. On early counting frames using beads, no beads at all meant nought.

In terms of measurement the length of various parts of the human body, such as the hand and the foot, were the basis for calculation. A natural yard is formed by the distance from the centre of the chest to the middle of a fully extended arm, and the fathom has its origin in the distance from hand to hand across the chest with both arms extended.

Ancient science

In the ancient world of Egypt and Mesopotamia early scientific knowledge was to a great extent bound up with astronomy and mathematics. This is also true of what little we know of the early science of India and the Far East. There were simple systems for calculating with number symbols, and the Babylonians and Assyrians in particular made quite complicated predictions about the movements of planets and stars. There were also very early forms of calendars and primitive maps were drawn.

The real development of scientific thought began with the Greeks and it was they who transformed the scattered bits and pieces of knowledge inherited from their predecessors and gave them real meaning. Most early scientific discoveries were prompted by the practical needs of peoples' everyday lives, but the Greeks went beyond this and pursued knowledge for its own sake.

It is important to remember that the Greek love of science was based on a belief that a sense of order existed in the natural world. This meant that outside men's minds there were certain laws and rules which governed the

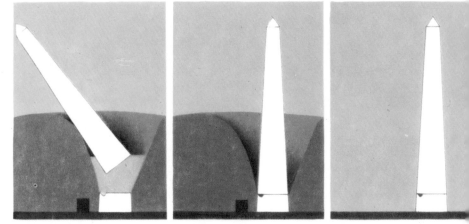

Top For a long time, archaeologists were curious to know how the ancient Egyptians managed to build the pyramids before lifting gear had been invented. The most likely explanation is that objects were hauled into position up ramps by thousands of slaves. Primitive cranes, like the one in the picture were probably also used to lift small weights.

Centre These pictures show how obelisks were erected without a crane. It was effected simply by digging a hole in the ground first and then partly filling it with sand. The obelisk was then tilted into the top of the hole and lowered into position as the sand was removed from the bottom.

Left Archimedes, the Greek mathematician who lived during the 3rd century BC, made a great discovery when climbing into his bath. It was that an object placed in water will displace a volume of water, the weight of which is equal to its own weight.

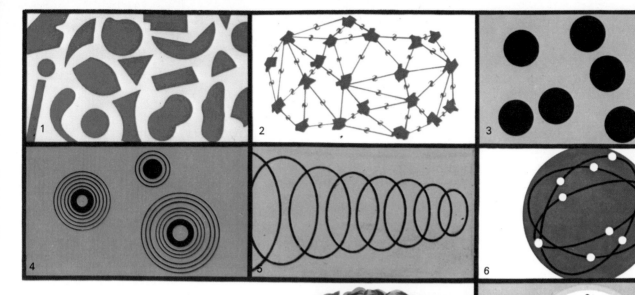

universe. The aim of Greek philosophers, who were also the scientists of their day, was to discover how and why these laws worked. They wanted to know these things for no other reason than that they existed. The solution to every new problem was one further step to an understanding of the whole nature of the world in which man lived.

Today, although the scientist still seeks out knowledge for its own sake, the time, money and equipment are often made available to him by government and organisations which have positive ends in view. These may be to do with the improvement of an industrial process or the invention of a new weapon of war or a means of defence.

One of the earliest Greek men of science was Thales, who lived in Asia Minor at a place called Miletus in the 7th and 6th centuries BC. He is said to have made an accurate prediction of an eclipse of the sun in 585 BC which caused a stir. For here was a philosopher forecasting a mysterious event, which people had always seen as an act of the gods, as though it were the solution to a mathematical problem. Thales developed the Egyptians' knowledge of geometry and put his findings to practical use, such as measuring the height of a pyramid by comparing the length of its shadow with the length of the shadow cast by a pole of known height.

There were many theories about the way in which the universe was made up. These theories tried to reduce

Above **Democritus, a Greek philosopher who lived during the 5th century BC. He advanced a theory of atoms, believing – as we do today – that everything is made up of atoms. But he thought that the atom could not be divided.**

Top **These diagrams describe the way thinkers through the ages have explained the structure of matter. Democritus said that things consisted of atoms which looked like those in (1). Epicurus agreed with him but thought that the atoms in solids were all hooked together as in (2). The next theory of atoms was put forward by Newton in the 17th century. Figure (3) shows his pattern of atoms, kept together by magnetism or some other force. In (4) we see the theory advanced by Dalton who said that atoms were each surrounded by heat. Kelvin believed they were spirals of electricity (5). Figure (6) shows Thomson's theory of a ball of electricity completely encircled by a structure of electrons. In 1911, Rutherford claimed that the atom was a nucleus in a ball of electrons (7).**

everything to a formula, so that matter and all the things made from it, including man himself, was thought to be composed of certain basic elements, such as fire, water and air. Democritus, who lived from about 470 to 400 BC, formed an atomic theory (revived by modern scientists) which laid down that all things are made up of atoms and the space which divides them. He thought of atoms as the smallest particles of matter, and the Greek word *atomos* means indivisible.

Pythagoras and his followers made many discoveries to do with the 'harmony' of numbers. They tried to show that nature was based on certain numerical ratios and proportions. These were sometimes expressed as geometric principles, such as the famous one: that the square on the side opposite to the right-angle of a triangle is equal to the sum of the squares on the other two sides. But numerical harmony was also found to exist in such things as music, painting and architecture. Because Pythagoreans believed the number 10 to be perfect, and only nine heavenly bodies were visible in the sky at the time, they even invented a 'counter-earth' to make up this 'perfect' number.

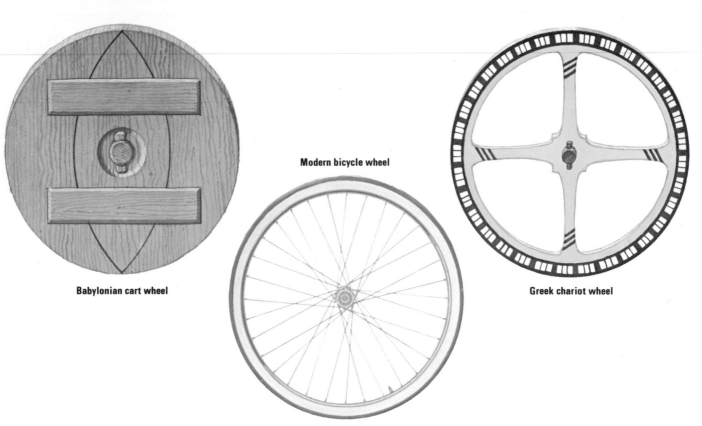

Babylonian cart wheel

Modern bicycle wheel

Greek chariot wheel

Above **Some examples of wheels: (left) a very old cart wheel from Mesopotamia; (right) a Greek chariot wheel with spokes; (centre) a wheel from a modern bicycle.**

The wheel

Imagine living in a lonely place with no trains, buses, cars, or bicycles. You would have to walk everywhere. This is what life was like in primitive times. Gradually, many thousands of years ago, men started to live in groups near rivers. They built huts to live in and began to grow crops in the land around their settlements. Men had learnt to be farmers. At first animals were used to carry men and their goods. With the invention of the wheel civilization took a tremendous leap forward. You can get an idea of the use of wheels by putting a heavy book on a table and pushing it along. Then take some round pencils and rest the book on them. It is now much easier to move the book by making the pencils roll

underneath it. We say that there is less *friction* when things roll, than when they slide. The large stones at Stonehenge were probably moved on tree trunk rollers.

Nobody knows who first had the idea of using wheels. In Asia, about 4000 B.C., men had carts with wheels that were solid circles of wood. Two wheels on either side of the cart were joined by a pole which we now call the *axle*. The axle was joined to the cart. These carts were first pushed by men. Later they were pulled by horses.

By 1750 B.C., the Ancient Egyptians were using spokes on their wheels. The spokes came out of the *hub* at the centre of the wheel. They were attached to an outer rim which moved over the ground. The wheels, made of wood, were much lighter than the older, solid wheels. Vehicles could therefore move

Below **It is much easier to push a book along on rollers. This is because the surfaces in contact roll over one another rather than sliding and this involves less friction.**

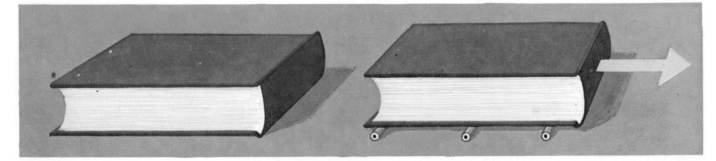

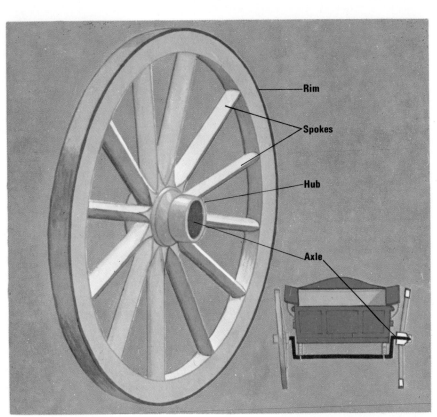

Rim

Spokes

Hub

Axle

much faster. Egyptian chariots had spoked wheels and were greatly feared by opposing armies because of the speed at which they could move. Instead of wood, the Romans used iron to make their spoked wheels; they therefore lasted much longer but were very heavy.

When a wheel is turning it moves on the axle, which goes through a hole in its centre. The point where the axle goes through the wheel is called the *bearing*. When the wheel moves, the axle is fixed and the hub of the wheel rubs against the axle. This friction makes it more difficult for the wheel to go round and the parts quickly wear out. It also makes the hub and axle very hot when the wheel turns quickly.

To make it easier for the hub to slide on the axle it is coated with grease or oil. Early man probably used animal fats for this.

Ballbearings were first used in the nineteenth century. They are used in many modern wheels. A number of steel balls are held between the inside of the hub and the axle. Instead of sliding on the axle the hub rolls around it, just as the book moves along the rollers. Because the balls roll instead of sliding, the wheel turns more easily.

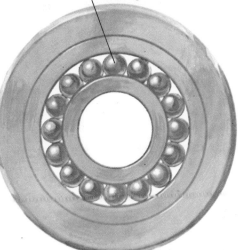

Ball bearings

Above **When rubber was invented it was a better material than iron for making tyres. The tyres on this penny-farthing are made of solid rubber.**

Above left **The first wheels were made of wood. In the sixteenth century the first tyre was made. This was a band of iron in the shape of a hoop, which was made to fit tightly around the wheel. These wheels were lighter than solid iron wheels and lasted almost as long. Wheels were also made with a saucer shape. They were held on the cart as shown in the diagram. This made them stronger. They were called** *dished wheels.*

Left **An aeroplane tyre. This is an example of a pneumatic tyre (first invented in 1845). Pneumatic means filled with air. The air is pumped into the tyre through an opening with a special stopper called a valve. The air inside makes the wheel more bouncy than one with a solid tyre. Most vehicles have pneumatic tyres nowadays. The pattern cut into the rubber is called the tread. It prevents the aeroplane skidding when it takes off or lands.**

Left **Ballbearings make the wheel move more easily on the axle.**

Primitive people carried their burdens on poles or dragged them along the ground. Canoes were carved out of fallen tree trunks found near the rivers.

Transport

One of man's earliest needs was to find a way of transporting himself and his belongings on land from one place to another. This was particularly so at the time before man became a farmer, when he lived a nomadic, or wandering, life. At first, he travelled on foot and carried everything with him on his back. At least, the womenfolk did, since it was generally necessary for men to keep their hands free to use their weapons to defend themselves against wild beasts or other men.

Probably the earliest form of transport was some kind of sledge made very simply of two trailing sticks fastened together with cross-pieces. This contraption would originally have been hauled by man himself, but later the idea of harnessing the sledge to an animal would have occurred.

The greatest single invention in the whole history of transport is the wheel. No one knows how it was first thought of, but it is most likely that it developed from the wooden rollers or tree trunks used in ancient times to move large blocks of stone.

In the world in which primitive man lived, water was a great natural element, and sooner or later he would have wished to travel across it. Whether it be to traverse the seas or simply to reach from one bank of a river to another his need was the same: something which would float and support the human body. One theory is that man used instinctively a fallen tree trunk or branch to assist him while he swam in the water. From this, it was an easy step to the moment when he clambered on to the log and

Above **A sedan chair, popular transport in the 18th century.**

used it as a simple boat. Fallen tree trunks may also have formed the first bridges.

When man actually began to make boats he used the material that lay to hand around him. In wooded areas trees were fashioned into dugout canoes, whereas in other places the dried skins of animals were stretched across rough wooden frames to make canoes or kayaks.

In the ancient world transport across land on a horse, or some other animal, or in a kind of vehicle hauled by an animal, was the privilege of the few. Most people walked, and for this reason few moved about very much except within the confines of their own home and village. Unless, of course, you happened to be in the army: one thinks of the epic journeys on foot of Alexander's soldiers, or of the 10,000 Greek mercenaries who walked 1,500 miles *2413 kilometres* back from Babylon to the Black Sea after a battle.

The first roads were tracks worn by men or animals. These might have been simply short cuts through a forest from one village compound to another, or the mighty trade routes, hundreds of miles long, worn down by the constant traffic of merchants. The first bush trails in Africa followed the paths of animals, and it is interesting to know that the route for the Canadian Pacific Railway through the Rocky Mountains in Canada follows the course of ancient passes discovered and trodden by thousands of American bison.

Below **Camels are called 'ships of the desert' because they are used as beasts of burden in desert areas. They have great powers of endurance, being able to withstand intense heat and cold and they can live without water for several days.**

Left **An Indian elephant carrying a maharajah on a ceremonial occasion.**

Above **The stage coach was a familiar sight in 18th- and 19th-century England.**

Below **Rickshaws were often used in the Far East to carry people about.**

Above **A cart like this was a common mode of transport until the coming of the motor.**

Above **A horse-drawn passenger train. The first railway, opened in 1803, was like this but it carried only goods. It was not long before steam locomotives were taking over from the horses.**

Travel by rail

The earliest records of railways date from about the 16th century. In the mining districts of central Europe wheeled carts hauled by horses used to carry coal. Their wheels wore ruts into the ground and to strengthen these ruts someone had the idea of laying strips of timber along them: in this way the first rails were invented. The standard gauge of track used in the first iron railways in Britain was probably determined by the average width of the old coal carts. The gauge also corresponds roughly to the width of a Roman chariot and it is possible that railed tracks of this sort existed in the ancient world. Cast-iron rails date from the 1760s and sleepers, made from stone and later from wood, were in use before the steam engine appeared.

The first true public railway was the Surrey Iron Railway in southern England which was opened in 1804. It carried only goods, and its wagons were hauled by horses. In the same year the first steam locomotive to run on rails, built by the English engineer, Richard Trevithick, was tried out at Pen-y-darran in Wales.

The most famous of all railway engineers, George Stephenson and his son Robert, developed the first successful railways to transport passengers as well as goods. George Stephenson was appointed engineer to the Stockton and Darlington Railway and he persuaded the directors of the company to use locomotives powered by steam engines as well as horses. He and Robert founded their own company to build the locomotives. Despite much opposition from the public and a general disbelief in the efficiency of the steam

Above **George and Robert Stephenson's famous 'Rocket'. In 1829, the Liverpool and Manchester Railway offered a prize of £500 in a competition for the best steam locomotive. 'Rocket' won as it pulled a full load at an average speed of 24 m.p.h.** *38.5 k.p.h.*

Below **The 'Catch-me-who-Can' railway invented by Richard Trevithick in 1808. The public would pay a shilling to ride on a circular track in an open carriage.**

engine, the opening of the Stockton and Darlington Railway in 1825 was a great success. The engine, *Locomotion No. 1*, driven by George Stephenson himself, hauled no less than thirty-eight wagons at a speed of 15 m.p.h. *24 k.p.h.*

In 1829 the celebrated Rainhill Trials were held to decide which locomotive should have the honour of pulling the trains on the new railway from Liverpool to Manchester.

The winner was the most famous of all railway engines, George and Robert Stephenson's *Rocket*. The Liverpool and Manchester Railway became the first complete railway in the world, in the sense that it ran regular scheduled services and was entirely steam-hauled from the beginning. Those who attended the opening ceremony witnessed the first fatal rail accident, when William Huskisson, who was a member of parliament for Liverpool, was run over and killed by the *Rocket*.

Very soon after the first locomotives were running successfully in England, railways powered by steam began to operate in other parts of the world. The Stephensons were responsible for the design of many of the first engines exported from Britain to other parts of Europe and the United States. In 1829 Marc Seguin built the first French locomotive, while in the United States the first steam-powered locomotive to run on rails was built by John Stevens in 1825.

Below This picture shows how some engines had strange designs at the beginning of the railway era. Here is 'The Best Friend of Charleston', the first steam locomotive to run on a regular service in the United States in 1830.

Left An American locomotive of the last century. It shows the 'cow catcher' on the front which prevented buffaloes from falling beneath the wheels. It was the coming of the railways in America that enabled large tracts of land to be developed by settlers.

Above A Post Office van which made its appearance on the London and Birmingham Railway in 1838. The basket on the side was for picking up mail bags without stopping the train. Carrying the mail has been an important part of the work of the railways since 1830. Eight years later, letters were being sorted in the mail van as the train sped along the track.

Left **The reconstruction of an Egyptian ship which was in service about 1300 BC. It is based on a model found in the tomb of Tutankhamen. As the picture shows, it is a sailing ship steered by two oars at the stern acting as rudders.**

The first great sea-faring and trading people, the Phoenicians, founded colonies all along the shores of the Mediterranean, yet there is little known about their ships. The Greeks and Romans had large merchant fleets, but the most familiar ships from these civilisations are the war galleys, light and elegant in Greek days, and sturdy and powerful in Roman times.

From the waters of northern Europe the seamen of Scandinavia explored the world in their longships. There was little contact with the people of Mediterranean countries and the boats of the Norsemen developed

Travel by sea

Many early forms of boats continue to be made and used in various parts of the world where people still live in primitive conditions. The earliest boats with sails, oars and rudders of which we have a record are those of the ancient Egyptians. Models of ships which journeyed up and down the Nile have been found in tombs of the pharoahs dating from about 2000 BC. Drawings from an even earlier period suggest that the Egyptians had properly built boats of a crude sort as long ago as 4000 BC. But the shape and design of boats altered very little in the ancient world.

independently. It is now believed that the Vikings crossed the Atlantic in their open boats to land on the shores of North America in about the year AD 1000, nearly 500 years before Columbus 'discovered' the continent.

Above **A Greek war galley. The fighting platform can be seen on the side above the oars.**

Left **'Henry Grace à Dieu', a massive warship armed with 186 guns, built by Henry VIII in 1514 to meet the ever-growing challenge of Spain.**

Above **Ships' figureheads were believed to contain spirits who acted as the ships' eyes for protection. This one is on the 'Cutty Sark'.**

Sea-power was important in the Middle Ages, as the Danes and others who invaded England and central Europe demonstrated. King Alfred built the first English navy, which was so neglected after his death that in 1066 William the Conqueror was able to land his great fleet of warships and transports on the shores of England with little opposition.

During medieval times ships in northern Europe began to rely entirely on the power of sail, and high castle-like platforms developed fore and aft. In the Mediterranean, galleys continued to be used and it was not until the 16th century that these oar-propelled vessels died out. The last important sea battle in which galleys played a major part was the Battle of Lepanto between the Turks and the forces of the Christian League in 1571.

The voyages of discovery into the New World, around Africa, and far away to the East, were made in three-masted carracks and caravels which, despite their smallness, mastered the perils of the oceans. Voyages such as the three-year expedition of Magellan's fleet around the world are a wonderful tribute to the ship-builders

Above **Capt. Cook's 'Endeavour'. In 1768, Cook sailed this ship to the South Seas to observe the movement of the planet, Venus, for the Royal Society. He returned by the unknown eastern coastline of Australia and charted it brilliantly.**

Above **An old American frigate, 'The President'. A frigate's main function was to find the enemy and to report its position to the battle fleet.**

Below **The 'Cutty Sark' the famous tea clipper built for the tea trade in 1869. She made several record runs between Australia and England.**

of Portugal, Spain and the Netherlands, who led the way in these epic journeys.

The English warships of Henry VIII's fleet were the first to mount cannon effectively between the decks and fire them through portholes. This revolutionary step led to the great sea battles of the Elizabethan era which ended in the dramatic defeat of the Spanish Armada by the small, manoeuvrable ships of England. Over the course of about 250 years ships grew bigger but did not alter greatly in design. The tactics of sea warfare continued to be based on the effective use of wind and sail and maximum fire power from broadsides of cannon.

The last great days of sail belonged to the graceful frigates and clippers of the 18th and 19th centuries, until the power of steam was harnessed to a ship for the first time.

No one man can be credited with the design of the first steamship. There were many early experiments in Europe and the United States in the 18th century but the first effective steamboat is generally taken to be the *Charlotte Dundas* built in Britain by William Symington in 1801. The boat was not given a fair trial and progress switched to the United States where Robert Fulton, who was much interested in the design of submarines, successfully launched the *Clermont*, a steamship powered by a Boulton and Watt engine.

Probably the most famous steamships of the 19th century were three vessels built by I. K. Brunel. These were the *Great Western*, the first steamship to be built specially for service between Europe and America; the *Great Britain*, the first iron-built transatlantic liner with screw propellers; and the mighty *Great Eastern*,

Above **The 'Savannah' which came into service when sails were giving way to steam.**

Above **The deep south of the USA once had unusual theatres called showboats. These were floating music halls which plied the Mississippi river. Here is the 'Robert E. Lee', the most famous showboat.**

Below **The 'Campania', an early aircraft carrier used in the First World War. The picture shows a Sopwith Pup circling before landing on the flight deck in front of the bridge.**

launched in 1858, then the largest vessel ever built, over five time bigger than anything that had gone before. She was intended to be the finest passenger-carrying ship in the world, but was a failure. Her size made a smooth passage difficult and many of the world's ports could not accommodate so vast a ship. She finished her days as a cable-layer and was scrapped in 1888.

Fighting ships continued to be made of wood until the middle of the 19th century. The first iron-clad battleship was the *Devastation*, built in Britain in 1873. The two world wars brought great advances in the design of ships. Before the coming of the aeroplane, command of the seas was supremely important and all the big powers in the First World War had powerful fighting fleets. Although command of the air became more important in the Second World War the development

Left **A modern aircraft carrier – the US Navy's 'Enterprise'. The deck is large enough for fast jets to land on it and many hundreds of planes can be housed below decks.**

of underwater craft was vital. Britain, during a period when she fought alone, was nearly starved out of existence because of the destruction wrought upon her merchant convoys by submarines.

Between the wars the great transatlantic liners battled for the Blue Riband, an award made for the fastest trip between Europe and North America. The last of these enormous luxury liners was the 80,000-ton *Queen Elizabeth*, launched in 1938.

Nuclear power is now being used to propel ships on and under the seas, and one of its great advantages is the fact that a vessel is able to stay at sea for long periods without refuelling.

Above right **A modern cruise liner, the 'Nordic Prince'.**

Far right **A container ship fully loaded. Modern container ships are capable of carrying many thousands of tons of cargo.**

Below **A cross section of a container ship showing the engines, crew's cabins and bridge.**

Travel by road

Below **This was the first successful petrol-driven car. It was invented by Siegfried Marcus in 1874. Though it could be driven under its own power it was heavy and clumsy. It was not a commercial success.**

Below, bottom **In 1873, Bollée's L'Obéissante was the first car to have pivoting front wheels, instead of the whole axle moving. This meant that it was more easily steered and manoeuvred. The car was very elaborate. Its steam engine was placed at the back. The wheels were moved by the steam in much the same way as pedals move a bicycle – by turning gear wheels.**

Bottom right **The 1911 Ford Model T was the most popular car made at the time. Between 1908–1927, fifteen million were sold.**

After Newcomen had invented the steam engine in 1712, attempts were made to harness this device to a cart in place of the horse. It was only with Watt's improved engine that this became possible. The first successful power-driven cart was built in 1769 by Nicholas Cugnot. From then on, all over the world a great variety of extraordinary steam-powered vehicles were produced.

The first practical steam vehicles, called 'horseless carriages', were built in 1820. Good roads, had been built by Telford and Macadam for horse-drawn vehicles. The hard surfaces were ideal for steam carriages.

The early vehicles resembled stage coaches and carried goods and passengers in the same way. They travelled at about 30mph (48kph). However, in the 1865 Road Locomotives Act (called the Red Flag Act), the Government restricted their speed to 4mph ($6\frac{1}{2}$kph). This Act slowed down car development in Britain very considerably.

In the nineteenth century, the trend was to develop light vehicles, which were easy to manoeuvre. One problem with a steam engine is that it requires a furnace of some sort to raise steam, and this means carrying large quantities of heavy and bulky coal–like an old-fashioned steam engine. With the development of the oil industry, inflammable liquids such as petrol and paraffin made it possible to do away with external combustion in engines. In their place internal-combustion engines were built, in which the petrol vapour explodes inside the cylinder.

The first successful petrol engine was built by Etienne Lenoir in 1860. This inspired a German, N. A.

Marcus petrol car

L'Obéissante

Ford Model 'T'

Right **The Panhard Levassor Saloon Car of 1895, the first to have its engine at the front.**

90

Otto, to build a 'four stroke' internal-combustion engine in 1876.

The world's first practical petrol-driven cars were produced in 1885. In 1889 petrol cars were imported into Britain and the speed limit was raised to 12mph (19kph).

At the beginning of the twentieth century more steam engine cars were produced. In 1906 the Stanley brothers in America produced the *Stanley Rocket* capable of travelling at 127mph. However, steam cars disappeared as they were clumsy and expensive to run.

The main development was switched to petrol-driven cars, the important improvements occurring in the period 1907–1930. In 1907, Sir Henry Royce produced his first famous *Silver Ghost*. In this period car bodies became stronger and more streamlined. Front suspension was added and syncromesh gears were invented. Shock absorbers, windscreen wipers, and indicators became standard equipment on every car. Since 1930 major developments include the use of automatic gears and the invention of the Wankel engine.

The first electric cars appeared in 1890, made possible by Gaston Plant's invention of a storage battery. Though popular, they could only go short distances before the battery needed recharging. When petrol cars became self-starting, electric cars went out of favour, though they are still used today for milk floats and other delivery vehicles. Interest in electric cars has revived because they do not cause pollution and it is hoped that new lighter types of batteries or fuel cells can be developed to last a similar time as a full tank of petrol.

Below **The Wankel engine has a rotating piston in place of the two-stroke piston which moves up and down. The principle on which both engines work is similar, but in the Wankel engine the triangular-shaped piston compresses the air and petrol mixture within an elliptical cylinder.**

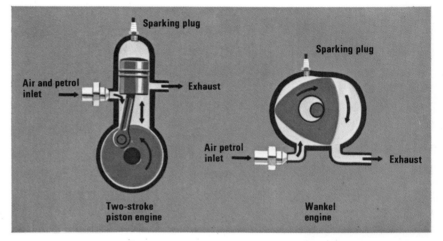

Sparking plug · Sparking plug · Air and petrol inlet · Exhaust · Air petrol inlet · Exhaust · Two-stroke piston engine · Wankel engine

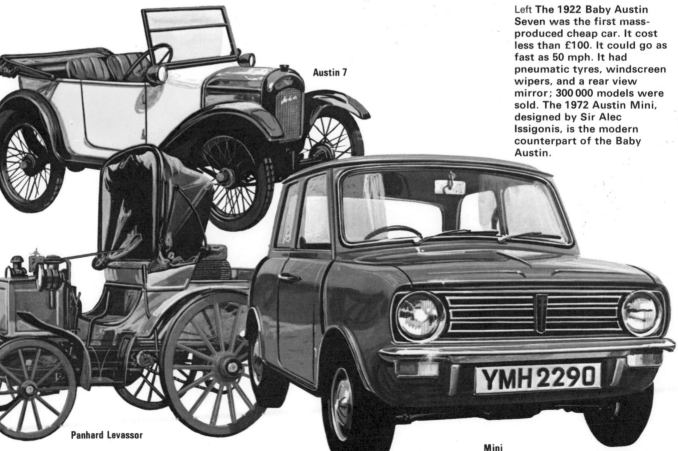

Austin 7

Panhard Levassor

Mini

YMH 2290

Left **The 1922 Baby Austin Seven was the first mass-produced cheap car. It cost less than £100. It could go as fast as 50 mph. It had pneumatic tyres, windscreen wipers, and a rear view mirror; 300 000 models were sold. The 1972 Austin Mini, designed by Sir Alec Issigonis, is the modern counterpart of the Baby Austin.**

Travel by air

Man has dreamed of flying ever since he first looked up into the sky and watched the easy progress of the birds through the air. At first he did not think of flying as a means of transport but as a spiritual experience, a release from the earth-bound troubles of his life. This is understandable since he looked upon the sky as the natural home of the gods. Although flying was one of man's earliest basic desires it is only in the last 70 years that science has come to his aid and helped him construct machines which permit him to travel safely in the air.

Most early attempts at flying were doomed to failure because men tried to imitate the flapping wings of birds. Leonardo da Vinci designed a machine to be propelled by the arms and legs,

Above An 11th-century British monk thought he could fly by using bird's feathers and flapping his arms about.

Right Centuries ago, inventors thought that 'sky ships' would be like those on the sea. Here are two of them – the one with balloons was invented by Francesco de Lana in 1670. The other is the 'Convertiplane' designed in 1843 by Sir George Cayley, a Yorkshire squire.

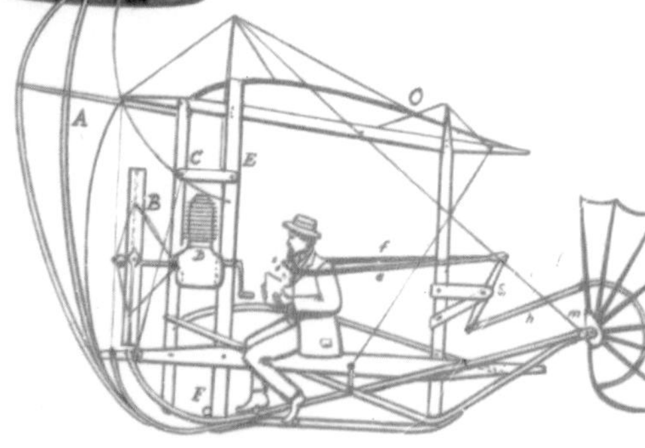

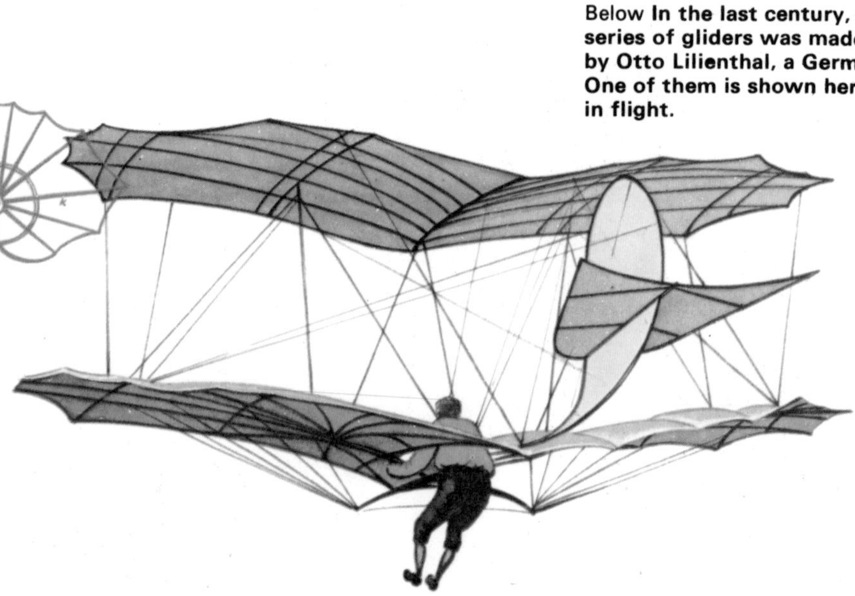

although he realised that a heavier-than-air machine could not be kept in flight by physical effort alone. The first successful experiments to lift people off the ground were with lighter than-air machines, or balloons.

The fixed-wing model gliders designed by Sir George Cayley in England in the early 19th century gave the first practical demonstrations of the true principles of flight. Then in 1891, Otto Lilienthal, the German 'bird-man', built his first glider. He went on to make over 2,000 remarkable flights over short distances in single and double fixed-wing

Top A Montgolfière hot-air balloon which made the first manned flight over Paris in 1783.

Above Part of the original plan of Wolfmüller's flying machine showing the elevator.

Below In the last century, a series of gliders was made by Otto Lilienthal, a German. One of them is shown here in flight.

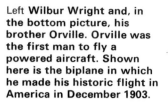

Left **Wilbur Wright and, in the bottom picture, his brother Orville. Orville was the first man to fly a powered aircraft. Shown here is the biplane in which he made his historic flight in America in December 1903.**

Below **(1) The monoplane in which Bleriot crossed the Channel; (2) a Tiger Moth Trainer and (3) a Jungmeister.**

Americans, Orville and Wilbur Wright, made four flights, the last of which covered 852 feet *259 metres*: a short enough distance for such an enormously important event.

The progress in the practical application of the science of aeronautics since that date has been astonishing. Even allowing for the fact that two world wars brought unusual pressures to bear on inventors – and unlimited funds – to move from the flimsy struts and wires of the *Flyer* to the supersonic aircraft of today is a vast leap in a period of 70 years.

When one looks at the sleek shapes of modern aircraft it is difficult to understand how designers managed to produce so many of the weird and unlikely-looking aircraft which followed the Wright brothers' achievement. But some of them, such as the French *Antoinette* monoplane of 1911, are elegant and graceful machines.

aircraft which he controlled by movements of his body.

The historical moment when man made his first sustained flight in an aeroplane powered by an engine took place on 17 December 1903 at Kittyhawk in the United States. In the *Flyer* driven by a 12 h.p. engine the

The daring and skill of the early pioneers were soon put to the test during the First World War. The aeroplane grew up almost overnight from a design experiment into a deadly weapon of war. Apart from its immense importance as a fighting machine, the aeroplane has also quickly established its place as the chief means of long-distance transport. The first passenger airlines were formed in the 1920s, and today the network of their routes penetrates into the remotest corners of the world. Now the scientist and the explorer have moved on from aeroplanes to rockets and seek to journey to other planets.

Index